Where's The Church?

By

Barry G Wallis

Library of Congress Control Number (LCCN): 2026905827

ISBNs:
eBook: 979-8-90224-152-2
Paperback: 979-8-90224-153-9
Hardback: 979-8-90224-154-6

Published by:
Authors Publishing House
178 Broadway, 3rd Floor,
New York, NY 10001, USA

Main Line: (855) 624-0155
Email: support@authorspublishinghouse.com

Table of Content

Thesis: In a world groaning under the weight of suffering, the Church must rediscover its identity—not as a building, but as the living hands and feet of Christ.

- **Lisa's Story**: A modern parable of abandonment, spiritual betrayal, and the tragic cost of ecclesiastical indifference.

- **Provocation**: "*Where's The Church*?"—not as a rhetorical jab, but as a divine summons.

- Contrast between theological orthodoxy and practical compassion

- James 2:16 and 1 John 3:17 as litmus tests of authentic faith

- How institutional filters (job type, attendance, appearance) distort grace

- The danger of moral gatekeeping over mercy

- Matthew 28:19–20 vs. the absence of discipleship in crisis

- The Church's failure to "go" beyond its walls

Foreword

This book was born from a question that refuses to stay quiet: *"Where's the Church?"*

It is asked in hospital waiting rooms and food pantry lines.

It is whispered by foster children and shouted by protestors.

It is written in the margins of society—where pain is raw, hope is fragile, and presence is rare.

It is not a question of theology. It is not a question of branding. It is a question of proximity.

Of embodied love. Of incarnational witness.

I did not author this book to criticize the Church.

I wrote it to call her forth.

To remind her who she is.

To summon her back to the places Jesus walked—the mess, the margins, the mourning.

You will not find easy answers on these pages. You will find stories. Scripture. Lament. Hope - And a prophetic invitation to show up.

Each chapter is a doorway. A threshold into deeper compassion. A summons to live the Gospel not just in word, but in witness.

This book is for weary pastors. For members who are wondering. For seekers who are searching. For prophets who are praying.

It is for anyone who has ever asked, *"Where's the Church?"* And for everyone who is ready to say, *"Here we are."*

May these words stir your spirit.

May they break your heart in holy ways.

May they move your feet toward the forgotten.

And may they remind you that when the Church shows up, Jesus is revealed.

And when Jesus is revealed, hope is reborn.

With urgency, joy, and love,

Barry G. Wallis

Introduction
The Echoing Question

Questions that die away with time — and there are questions that will not be hushed.

"Where's the Church?" is one of them.

It is not resounding through ivory towers and theology classes. It is an escalation of hospital exit ramps and eviction. It shivers in parents who have prayed all night long and still wake up to find empty cupboards. It haunts those who once believed in all things, those who served their purpose, and even those who, even yet, found themselves lonely when life was getting out of hand.

Critics of Christianity do not ask this question.

It is requested by people who believe in it.

The injured, the neglected, the wearied, and the true believer who found--it is frequently after it is too late--that faith without action is as hurtful as unbelief.

Church was never supposed to be a concept that we justify.

It was supposed to be an existing presence.

Since its inception, the Church has never been identified by its structures, finances, or power, but by its closeness to suffering. It moved toward pain. It crossed boundaries. It gave to the hungry, received the stranger, touched the untouchable, and bore each other's burdens. People did not attend the Church, they experienced it.

However, at some point in the process, something changed.

The Church in most places knew how to assemble--but had forgotten how to get away.

It had learnt how to preach--but had forgotten how to practice.

It had taught itself to defend itself--but had forgotten how to empty itself out.

This book is not intended to criticize the Church.

The reason why it is written is that the Church is too important not to tell the truth.

" Where's the Church?" is not an excommunication — it is an appeal. A reminder to keep in mind who we are and whose we are. A call to the revival of a faith that makes its appearance in times when prayers do not suffice, when sermons cannot suffice, and the presence of God alone is left as gospel.

The story is the heart of this book, not because it is unique, but because it is a tragic experience that is all too familiar. The case of Lisa is not told to inspire anger, but to open the eyes. It reveals the disastrous disparity between the Church confession and the world reality. It addresses us with the price of silence, indecisiveness, and wrong priorities.

This introduction is a provocation to take up the question rather than pass it over. To resist defensiveness. So that suffering may do its sacred task. Since renewal is not initiated by answers, it is initiated by honesty.

The subsequent chapters will deconstruct presumptions, reveal gaps, and bring the Church back to its prime ministry not as a dispensation of grace but the incarnation of it. Not as idolatry, but as an act of love.

According to the Church being the Body of Christ, His hands must continue to heal, His feet must continue to go, and His heart must continue to break what breaks the heart of God.

We should ask first how to repair the Church before we have the courage to hear the question that lacerated lives and holy places must answer:

Where is the Church?

And more importantly--

Are we ready to answer it?

Thesis: Where's The Church?

In a world groaning under the weight of suffering—where despair is not a distant concept but a daily companion for millions—the Church stands at a crossroads. The cries of the broken are not faint echoes from far-off lands; they rise from our neighborhoods, our schools, our shelters, and even our pews. They are the cries of single mothers choosing between groceries and rent, of veterans sleeping under bridges, of children growing up without hope, and of families like Lisa's—faithful, desperate, and abandoned.

And yet, amid this groaning, a haunting question reverberates through the silence:

Where is the Church?

Not the building with a steeple.

Not the programs printed in bulletins.

Not the polished sermons or the padded pews.

But the *Church*—the living, breathing body of Christ.

The people called to embody His compassion, His justice, His mercy, and His mission.

We were never meant to be spectators in sanctuaries.

We were called to be **salt and light** in the streets.

We were never commissioned to build monuments to our comfort.

We were sent to **make disciples**, to **bind up the brokenhearted**, to **proclaim liberty to the captives**, and to **feed the hungry, clothe the naked, and visit the imprisoned**.

The Church must rediscover its identity—not as a static institution, but as a Spirit-empowered movement.

Not as a fortress to retreat into, but as a force to be reckoned with. Not as a Sunday gathering, but as a 24/7 embodiment of Christ's love in action.

This rediscovery is not optional. It is urgent.

Because when the Church forgets who she is, the world forgets who Jesus is.

And when the Church is absent, injustice thrives, hope withers, and lives—like Lisa's—are lost.

This book is a call to awaken.

To repent of our indifference.

To rise from our slumber.

To become again what we were always meant to be:

The hands that heal. The feet that go. The heart that breaks. The voice that speaks. The Church that shows up.

Because when the Church shows up—**Jesus shows up.**

And when Jesus shows up—***Hope is Reborn.***

Lisa's Story

There was a young woman with a bright future ahead of her – for the sake of anonymity, we will call her "Lisa." She married the love of her life and embarked upon their life together. They soon had saved enough money to buy a home and wanted to start a family. It wasn't long before they were blessed with their first child, a happy little boy. Within a year, they had twin girls who brought much joy into their lives. It wasn't long after that she gave birth to their fourth child, another daughter. They had it all – so it seems.

Their careers were stable, and they had adequate income to live and meet their needs. She managed the household well and put back as much savings as possible, but with inflation, this was at best a challenge. He took a part-time job to help support the family. Unfortunately, the company she worked for was sold, and she lost her job. They determined that if she remained at home while he held his full-time and part-time jobs, they would be fine. This worked well for the next couple of years.

One of the twins became ill, and the cost of medical care took a toll on their limited savings, yet they believed all would be well. With mostly depleted savings, they set about caring for their family. This is when tragedy struck. Her parents perished in a plane crash while heading on vacation.

Her husband, whom we will call "Bill," was raised in an orphanage and had no family of his own. His wife and only child was now orphans with no other close family.

could not help her since she had not been very faithful in attending over the past several months.

A stray dog attacked her youngest child in their front yard – and this required surgery – more expenses that she could not afford, and even still, the church would not help.

This story does not have a happy ending at all. The pressures of life mounting, she spiraled downward in her thoughts, with nowhere to turn. The twin who had cancer suddenly passed away from the stress of the chemo, and her insurance company had reached the limits of her small policy. She stopped paying the premiums for which it took one of her jobs to pay, and bought a small life insurance policy.

She went to the fire station and inquired if they took children in, if there was no one to take them, because she heard this was a safe drop-off place. Puzzled, they turned her away. She used the remaining balance in her checking account to take the children on a picnic, and they spent the day playing and laughing as best they could. That night, she dropped off the children with the sitter on her way to work.

*Returning home – she wrote this note addressed to "**Whoever Might Care."***

" I have tried to be a good wife and a good Mom. Over the past three years, I have even tried to remain faithful in church to teach my children about God. I've exhausted everything and become such a bother to the church that I no longer feel welcome in God's house. It seems that everyone is willing to pray for me, but no one is willing to help me

because my job is not Christian enough, or good enough, or doesn't meet some unwritten code that I am not aware of. I'm so exhausted – losing my husband, a daughter, and nothing left to care for my children. I have been turned down for so many jobs that I no longer feel anything and have resigned myself to the fact that I am not worthy of my children. Food stamps helped, but they don't cover medical bills, clothing, school supplies, or other necessities of life. I feel I've run out of options.

Last night, after crying all night long, I concluded that my children need a new mom who can really take care of them. My heart is so heavy today that I cannot pretend that everything will be okay anymore. If I prayed just once more, I would have to ask God this simple question: ***"Where's The Church?"*** *In Sunday school, I was told the church was the hands and feet of God, but my family has not witnessed this. To whoever reads this, I have a life insurance policy to help pay for someone to take care of my children. The elders at the church told me they couldn't help me when I went back this morning because they have building expenses to pay, so I have no other options. Signed "Lisa"*

We know what happened next from viewing the security video from the neighbor's house. She opened the garage, took out all the bikes, drove her car inside, and shut the garage door. When she was found late that night, she had rolled down the windows with the car running and ended her life.

She passed from this life, not realizing her life insurance would not pay out for suicide. The church acted shocked over this ***"event"*** *as they* *called it, and could not seem to understand. Leadership could not understand the question she asked in her final note addressed to:*

"Whoever Might Care" *contains the difficult question of –* **Where's The Church?**

Provocation: "Where's The Church?"

Not a Rhetorical Jab, but a Divine Summons

"Where's The Church?"

This is not a sarcastic critique hurled from the sidelines.

It is not a cynical jab aimed at organized religion.

It is not the bitter cry of someone who has given up on faith.

No—this is the voice of the wounded calling out for healing.

It is the voice of the abandoned asking for presence.

It is the voice of the crucified Christ echoing through the suffering of His people.

It is not a rhetorical question.

It is a **divine summons**.

A summons to awaken from apathy.

A summons to repent of comfort-driven Christianity.

A summons to return to the radical, sacrificial, incarnational love that defined the early Church.

This question is the Spirit's trumpet blast in a slumbering sanctuary.

It is the knock at the door of every heart that claims to follow Jesus.

It is the holy discontent that refuses to let us settle for sanitized religion while the world bleeds.

"Where's The Church?"

—when the hungry are turned away with a prayer but no bread.

—when the grieving are met with silence instead of presence.

—when the poor are judged for their jobs instead of helped in their need.

—when the broken are told to clean up before they come in.

This question is not meant to shame.

It is meant to **summon**.

To call forth the Bride of Christ from behind stained glass and into the streets.

To call forth the Body of Christ to move again—with compassion, with courage, with conviction.

It is the same call that thundered through Isaiah's lips:

"Here I am, Lord. Send me."

It is the same cry that stirred the early Church to sell their possessions and meet every need.

It is the same Spirit that moved Jesus to touch lepers, dine with sinners, and weep at tombs.

So when we hear the question—*"Where's The Church?"*—Let us not deflect.

Let us not defend.

Let us not delay.

Let us answer:

"Here we are, Lord. Send us."

Part I

The Mission We Forgot

Chapter 1
The Gospel We Preach vs. The Gospel We Live

In the heart of Christian theology lies a tension—one that has shaped centuries of doctrine, divided denominations, and defined discipleship: the relationship between faith and works. This tension is not a flaw in the gospel; it is a feature. It is not meant to confuse the believer, but to convict the Church. It is the sacred friction between belief and behavior, between confession and compassion, between what we say we believe and how we live it out.

From the Reformation's cry of sola fide—faith alone—to James' bold declaration that faith without works is dead, this tension has sparked theological debates and ecclesial divides. But beyond the seminaries and pulpits, it has real-world consequences. Because when the Church fails to reconcile the gospel, it proclaims with the gospel it practices, it becomes a hollow echo in a hurting world.

This is not merely a doctrinal dilemma—it is a missional crisis. The Church cannot credibly ask *"Where's the world going?"* if it cannot first answer *"Where are we going?"* And it cannot answer *"Where's the Church?"* with integrity unless it is willing to examine whether its faith is alive enough to move, to serve, to sacrifice.

The gospel we preach must be more than words—it must be flesh. It must walk into hospital rooms, sit beside the grieving, feed the hungry, and welcome the outcast. It must be visible in the hands that serve, the feet that go, and the hearts that break for what breaks God's heart.

Because if our theology does not lead to mercy, it is incomplete. If our doctrine does not lead to justice, it is distorted. And if our faith does not lead to works, it is dead.

The question *"Where's The Church?"* is not just a lament—it is a mirror. It reflects back to us the gap between our proclamation and our presence. And it invites us—not to defend our traditions—but to *rediscover our mission*.

To be the Church that not only believes in grace, but lives it.

Not only preaches love, but practices it.

Not only does He sing about Jesus, but He also walks like Him.

This is the reconciliation we must pursue.

Because the world is not asking for our creeds.

It is crying out for our compassion.

Faith: The Foundation of Salvation

Scripture is clear: salvation is by grace through faith. The Apostle Paul writes, "For it is by grace you have been saved through faith—and this is not from yourselves, it is the gift of God—not by works, so that no one can boast" (Ephesians 2:8–9). Faith is the doorway through which we enter the Kingdom. It is not earned, not bought, not achieved—it is received.

Faith, in its purest form, is trust in the finished work of Christ. It is the conviction that Jesus' death and resurrection are sufficient to reconcile us to God. It is the assurance of things hoped for, the evidence of things not seen (Hebrews 11:1). This is the gospel we preach: that salvation is a gift, not a wage.

Works: The Fruit of Salvation

But James, the brother of Jesus, offers a sobering counterbalance to the doctrine of faith alone:

"Faith by itself, if it is not accompanied by action, is dead" (James 2:17).

This is not a contradiction—***it is a completion***.

James is not dismantling Paul's teaching on grace; he is demanding its evidence.

He is not arguing that works earn salvation; he is declaring that salvation earns works.

Because true faith—living faith—always moves.

- It acts.
- It shows up.
- It cannot remain passive, silent, or invisible.

James is confronting a dangerous illusion: that belief without embodiment is enough.

He is calling out a hollow religiosity that professes Christ but refuses to reflect Him.

He is challenging the Church to stop hiding behind doctrine and start living out discipleship.

And Paul, far from disagreeing, affirms this truth in his letter to the Ephesians:

"We are God's workmanship, created in Christ Jesus to do good works, which God prepared in advance for us to do" (Ephesians 2:10).

Paul's emphasis on grace is foundational—but it is not final. He teaches that we are saved unto good works—not by them, but for them.

The Church must understand this distinction:

- Works are not the root of salvation—they are the fruit.
- They are not the cause of redemption—they are its consequence.
- They are not the price of grace—they are its proof.

When the Church fails to produce this fruit, it risks becoming a tree with no life. A lamp with no oil. A body with no breath.

Faith is not merely intellectual assent—it is incarnational obedience. It is the kind of belief that bends low to wash feet, that breaks bread with the hungry, that weeps with the grieving, and that stands with the oppressed. This is the kind of faith that Jesus modeled. This is the kind of faith the early Church embodied. And this is the kind of faith the world is waiting to see again.

Because when faith moves—Jesus moves. And when Jesus moves—*Hope is Reborn*.

Theological Harmony: Paul and James in Concert

The apparent contradiction between Paul and James dissolves when we understand their contexts—not as opposing voices, but as complementary instruments in the symphony of grace. Paul was confronting the bondage of legalism. He was speaking to those who believed that salvation could be earned through strict adherence to the Mosaic Law, who trusted in circumcision, ritual purity, and religious performance as the pathway to righteousness.

His message was revolutionary: "By grace you have been saved through faith… not by works" (Ephesians 2:8–9). Paul was tearing down the walls of self-righteous striving and pointing to the cross as the only door to salvation.

James, on the other hand, was confronting the danger of spiritual complacency. He was speaking to believers who professed faith but lived unchanged—who claimed to follow Christ but failed to reflect Him. His message was equally urgent: "Faith by itself, if it is not accompanied by action, is dead" (James 2:17). James was not adding works to the gospel—he was demanding evidence of it. He was calling out a hollow faith that had no hands, no feet, no fruit.

Together, Paul and James declare a unified truth:

- Faith saves. Works prove.
- Faith is the root. Works are the fruit.
- Faith is the seed. Works are the harvest.
- Faith is the flame. Works are the light it casts.

This harmony is not theological trivia—it is a spiritual necessity. Because when the Church preaches grace but withholds mercy, it betrays the gospel.

When it proclaims love but refuses to serve, it becomes a clanging cymbal—loud but lifeless (1 Corinthians 13:1).

When it teaches righteousness but ignores suffering, it loses its witness and forfeits its credibility.

The world is not looking for a Church that can quote Scripture.

It is longing for a Church that can embody it.

A Church that does not just preach about the Good Samaritan, but becomes him.

A Church that does not just sing about Jesus, but walks like Him.

This is the kind of Church that answers the question *"Where's The Church?"* with presence, not platitudes.

- With action, not avoidance.
- With mercy, not metrics.

Because the gospel is not just a message to be believed—it is a mission to be lived.

And when the Church lives it, the world sees Jesus…

Lisa's Story: A Gospel Disconnected

Lisa's story is not an indictment of theology—it is an indictment of application. Her church preached salvation but failed to embody compassion. They taught faith but withheld works. They prayed but did not act. And in doing so, they answered her question—**"Where's The Church?"**—*__with silence__*.

This is the danger of a gospel that lives only in pulpits and not in neighborhoods. A gospel that comforts the saved but forgets the suffering. A gospel that sings on Sunday but is silent on Monday.

A Call to Reconnect

The Church must reconnect its proclamation with its practice. It must preach salvation by faith and live salvation through works. It must be remembered that Jesus did not just teach—He touched. He did not just preach—He fed. He did not just save—He served.

Because the gospel we preach is only as powerful as the gospel we live.

Bibliography

1. Bible Hub. "Faith vs. Works." https://biblehub.com/topical/f/faith_vs._works.htm

2. GotQuestions.org. "What is the biblical understanding of faith vs. works?" https://www.gotquestions.org/faith-vs-works.html

3. Questions in Theology. "Faith vs Works: Paul vs James." https://questionsintheology.com/faith-vs-works-paul-vs-james/

Chapter 2
The Church as a Refuge or a Gatekeeper?

In every generation, the Church stands at a crossroads—faced with a defining choice:

To be a refuge for the broken or a gatekeeper of the righteous.

This choice is not abstract. It is not confined to theological debate or doctrinal nuance.

It is lived out in the everyday rhythms of ministry:

- In the way a pastor responds to a single mother asking for help.
- In the tone of a sermon addressing addiction, poverty, or mental illness.
- In the policies that determine who receives aid, who is welcomed, and who is deemed *"acceptable."*
- In the quiet decisions made behind closed doors about budgets, benevolence, and belonging.

This choice is not made once—it is made daily.

And far too often, the Church has *chosen gatekeeping over grace*.

Gatekeeping asks, "Do they deserve help?"

Grace asks, "How can we help?"

Gatekeeping says, "Let's protect our purity."

Grace says, "Let's extend our presence."

Gatekeeping builds walls.

Grace builds bridges.

When the Church becomes a gatekeeper, it begins to resemble the deeply religious systems Jesus confronted.

It becomes more concerned with appearances than with healing.

More invested in control than in compassion.

More focused on maintaining order than on manifesting mercy.

But Jesus did not die to create a gated community of the morally elite.

He died to open the floodgates of grace to the least, the last, and the lost.

He did not rise to empower gatekeepers—He rose to commission servants.

He did not ascend to build barriers—He ascended to send His Spirit into every broken place.

The Church was never meant to be a checkpoint.

It was meant to be a sanctuary.

A place where the wounded are welcomed, the weary are refreshed, and the sinner is embraced—not shamed.

When we choose gatekeeping, we may preserve our image, but we lose our impact.

We may protect our doctrine, but we betray our mission.

We may maintain our buildings, but we abandon our calling.

The question *"**Where's The Church?**"* is not just about visibility—it is about posture.

Are we standing at the door with arms folded, or are we running down the road with arms wide open?

Are we filtering people through our preferences, or are we receiving them through Christ's mercy?

Because the world is not asking for a perfect Church.

It is crying out for a present one.

A Church that does not just preach grace—but **practices it**.

A Church that does not just sing about love—but **lives it**.

Let us choose again.

Let us choose *refuge over rejection*.

Let us choose *mercy over metrics*.

Let us choose *grace over gatekeeping*.

Because when the Church opens its doors, Heaven opens its heart.

The Original Design: A Shelter for the Weary

Jesus did not establish His Church to be a fortress of moral superiority.

He did not envision a gated institution where only the polished and pious could enter.

He did not die to create a hierarchy of holiness, where the wounded were kept at arm's length until they were *"**clean enough**"* to belong.

No—Jesus built His Church to be a sanctuary.

A refuge for the weary.

A shelter for the wounded.

A home for the wandering.

His ministry was marked by *radical inclusion*.

He touched lepers—those society deemed untouchable (Mark 1:40–42).

He dined with tax collectors—those labeled traitors and sinners (Luke 5:29–32).

He defended adulterers—those condemned by law and culture (John 8:3–11).

He welcomed children—those overlooked and undervalued (Mark 10:13–16).

He did not ask for credentials.

He offered compassion.

Jesus did not wait for people to get their lives together before He loved them.

He loved them into healing.

He loved them into transformation.

He loved them into belonging.

This is the posture the Church was meant to reflect.

Not one of judgment, but of **mercy**.

Not one of exclusion, but of **embrace**.

Not one of suspicion, but of **solidarity**.

In Acts 2, we see the Church in its purest form.

The early believers shared everything they had, ensuring no one among them was in need (Acts 2:44–45).

They did not screen for worthiness.

They responded to the need.

They did not ask, "Do they deserve this?"

They asked, ***"What do they need?"***

The Church was not a gated community—it was a healing community.

A place where generosity flowed freely.

Where burdens were carried together.

Where grace was not rationed, but poured out.

This is the blueprint.

This is the design.

This is the heart of Christ for His Bride.

And yet, somewhere along the way, the Church began to drift.

From sanctuary to institution.

From compassion to control.

From open arms to closed doors.

But the call remains.

To return.

To rebuild.

To become the Church Jesus imagined again.

A Church that touches the untouchable.

Dines with the outcast.

Defends the condemned.

Welcomes the forgotten.

A Church that does not ask for credentials—only for hearts willing to receive love.

A Church that does not measure worthiness—but responds to need.

Because when the Church becomes a sanctuary again,

Jesus becomes visible again.

And when Jesus becomes visible,

Hope is Reborn.

The Drift Toward Gatekeeping

But over time, the Church began to drift. Instead of asking, "***How can we help?***" it began asking, "***Do they qualify***?" Instead of opening doors, it built thresholds. Instead of being known for mercy, it became known for moral policing.

Lisa's story is a tragic example. She came to the Church not for handouts, but for hope. She was willing to work, willing to sacrifice, willing to endure. But because her job did not meet the Church's standards, she was denied help. Because she missed services while caring for her sick child, she was deemed unfaithful. Because she did not fit the mold, she was left outside the gate.

This is not an isolated incident. Across the world, churches have turned away people based on appearance, employment, marital status, addiction history, or theological alignment. The very place that should be a refuge becomes a courtroom. And the verdict is often rejection.

Biblical Rebuke of Gatekeeping

Scripture is not silent about this. In 1 John 3:17, we read: "If anyone has material possessions and sees a brother or sister in need but has no pity on them, how can the love of God be in that person?"

James 2:16 adds: "If one of you says to them, 'Go in peace; keep warm and well fed,' but does nothing about their physical needs, what good is it?"

These verses are not suggestions—they are indictments. They expose the hypocrisy of a Church that prays for the poor but refuses to feed them. They confront the disconnect between spiritual rhetoric and physical response.

Jesus Himself warned against religious gatekeeping. In Matthew 23:13, He rebuked the Pharisees: "You shut the door of the kingdom of heaven in people's faces. You yourselves do not enter, nor will you let those enter who are trying to."

This is the danger when the Church becomes more concerned with purity than presence, more focused on policy than people.

The Call to Return

The Church must return to its original design—not the one shaped by centuries of institutional tradition, but the one etched into the heart of Christ. The design that welcomed the broken, fed the poor, comforted the grieving, and embraced the outcast. The design that did not measure people by their worthiness but responded to their wounds.

We must stop asking, "*Are they worthy*?"

And start asking, "*Are they hurting*?"

Because the Church was never called to be a gate—guarded, selective, and closed to those who do not meet the criteria.

It was called to be a path—open, accessible, and leading people toward healing, hope, and redemption.

Not a judge—but a healer.

Not a filter—but a fountain.

Not a fortress—but a field hospital.

When the Church becomes a refuge, it reflects Jesus—who came not for the healthy, but for the sick (Luke 5:31).

Who broke bread with sinners.

Who wept with the grieving.

Who touched the untouchable.

Who forgave the condemned.

Who carried the cross for those who could not carry themselves.

But when the Church becomes a gatekeeper, it reflects the Pharisees—those who burdened the people with rules but refused to lift a finger to help (Matthew 23:4).

Those who prized purity over mercy.

Those who questioned Jesus for healing on the Sabbath.

Those who missed the Messiah because they were too busy maintaining appearances.

And the world is watching.

Not to see how well we preach—but how well we love.

Not to see how pure our doctrine is—but how present our compassion is.

Not to see how big our buildings are—but how open our hearts are.

The world is not asking for perfection.

It is *pleading for presence.*

It is not looking for a Church that has all the answers.

It is longing for a Church that will sit in the questions, walk through the pain, and show up when no one else will.

Let us be that Church.

Let us be the Church that opens doors—not just on Sunday mornings, but every day of the week.

That breaks bread—not just in communion, but in community.

That binds wounds—not just with prayer, but with presence, provision, and practical love.

Let us be the Church that answers the question *"**Where's The Church**?"*

Not with silence.

Not with excuses.

Not with policies.

But with a resounding, Spirit-filled, mercy-driven cry:

*"**Here we are.**"*

Here we are—in the shelters, in the hospitals, in the prisons, in the streets.

Here we are—feeding, listening, healing, loving.

Here we are—being the hands and feet of Jesus.

Because when the Church shows up, Jesus shows up.

And when Jesus shows up, ***Hope is Reborn**.*

Bibliography

1. Holy Bible, New International Version. Scriptures cited: Acts 2:44–45; 1 John 3:17; James 2:16; Matthew 23:13.

2. Keller, Timothy. *Generous Justice: How God's Grace Makes Us Just*. Dutton, 2010.

3. Bonhoeffer, Dietrich. *Life Together*. Harper & Row, 1954.

4. Lupton, Robert D. *Toxic Charity: How Churches and Charities Hurt Those They Help*. Harper One, 2011.

5. Wright, N.T. *Simply Jesus: A New Vision of Who He Was, What He Did, and Why He Matters*. Harper One, 2011.

Chapter 3

The Great Commission vs. The Great Omission

Jesus' final words to His disciples were not a suggestion.

They were not a closing benediction or a farewell blessing.

They were a command.

A commissioning.

A divine mandate that would define the mission of the Church for all time.

"Go therefore and make disciples of all nations, baptizing them in the name of the Father and of the Son and of the Holy Spirit, teaching them to observe all that I have commanded you" *(Matthew 28:19–20, ESV).*

This is what we call the **Great Commission**—not because it is optional, but because it is ultimate.

It is the heartbeat of the Church's purpose.

It is the reason the Church exists—not to preserve tradition, but to proclaim transformation.

Not to gather for comfort, but to scatter for impact.

Not to build monuments, but to make disciples.

The Great Commission is not confined to pulpits or programs.

It is not reserved for missionaries or ministers.

It is a call to movement.

To multiplication.

To mission.

It is a call to go—into neighborhoods, into nations, into nursing homes, into shelters, into prisons, into schools, into streets.

It is a call to baptize—not just with water, but with belonging.

It is a call to teach—not just with words, but with lives that reflect the commands of Christ.

And yet, in many corners of the modern Church, this commission has been quietly replaced by something far more comfortable:

The Great Omission.

The *Great Omission* is not written in creeds or carved into stone.

It is lived in silence.

It is practiced in passivity.

It is embodied in the Church that gathers but does not go.

That sings but does not serve.

That preaches but does not disciple.

The Great Omission is the Church that has traded movement for maintenance.

Mission for meetings.

Multiplication for metrics.

It is the Church that has forgotten that Jesus did not say, "***Stay and be safe.***"

He said, "***Go and make disciples.***"

This omission is not just a failure of strategy—it is a failure of obedience.

It is not just a missed opportunity—it is a missed calling.

And it has consequences.

Because when the Church omits the Commission,

The world omits the Church.

And when the Church is absent,

So is the witness of Christ.

Let us repent of the Great Omission.

Let us reclaim the Great Commission.

Let us rise again—not as spectators, but as sent ones.

Not as keepers of comfort, but as carriers of the Kingdom.

Because the world is not waiting for another sermon.

It is waiting for a Church that will go.

That will discipline.

That will teach.

That will love.

And when the Church goes—Jesus goes.

And when Jesus goes—**hope is reborn**.

From "Go" to "Stay"

The Great Commission begins with a verb: **Go**.

It is not passive. It is not optional. It is not vague.

It is active, urgent, and outward-facing.

It is the divine imperative that calls the Church to movement—into neighborhoods, into nations, into the margins, into the mess.

But somewhere along the way, many churches *have traded "Go" for "Stay."*

Stay in our buildings.

Stay in our comfort zones.

Stay in our theological bubbles.

Stay in our routines.

We have become experts in gathering, but novices in going.

We know how to host conferences, but not how to walk with the broken.

We know how to plan worship sets, but not how to respond to suffering.

We have perfected the Sunday service, but neglected the Monday mission.

We have built sanctuaries, but forgotten the streets.

We have cultivated atmospheres of inspiration, but abandoned the call to incarnation.

This is not just a strategic misstep—it is a spiritual crisis.

This is the ***Great Omission***:

- The failure to go where Jesus would go.
- The failure to disciple beyond conversion.
- The failure to teach obedience—not just to doctrine, but to compassion, justice, and mercy.

We have taught people how to believe, but not how to love.

We have taught people how to attend, but not how to serve.

We have taught people how to quote Scripture, but not how to embody it.

Jesus did not say, ***"Stay and build bigger buildings."***

He said, ***"Go and make disciples."***

He did not say, ***"Stay and protect your purity."***

He said, ***"Go and touch the leper."***

He did not say, ***"Stay and preserve tradition."***

He said, ***"Go and proclaim the Kingdom."***

The Church must recover its movement.

Because the gospel is not static—it is kinetic.

It does not sit—it walks.

It does not wait—it reaches.

It does not hide—it heals.

And if we are to answer the question *"**Where's The Church**?"* with integrity,

We must first ask:

Where have we gone?

Have we gone to the hurting?

Have we gone to the hungry?

Have we gone to the forgotten?

Or have we stayed—safe, silent, and satisfied?

Let us repent of our staying.

Let us rise to our going.

Let us become again the Church that moves with mercy, walks with justice, and lives with love.

Because when the Church goes—Jesus goes.

And when Jesus goes—***hope is reborn**.*

Discipleship Deferred

Discipleship is not just about Bible study.

It is not merely the memorization of verses or the mastery of doctrine.

It is about transformation.

It is about walking with people—not just into the waters of baptism, but through the fires of life.

Through pain.

Through doubt.

Through addiction.

Through poverty.

Through grief.

Discipleship is not a classroom—it is a ***journey***.

It is not a lecture—it is a ***life shared***.

It is not a curriculum—it is ***a covenant***.

It is the sacred commitment to walk with someone as they learn to walk with Christ.

To model the life of Jesus—not just in belief, but in behavior.

To embody His compassion, His patience, His truth, His mercy, His endurance.

Jesus did not disciple with a syllabus.

He discipled with His presence.

He walked with His followers for three years—through storms, through betrayals, through miracles, through meals.

He taught them not just with words, but with wounds.

Not just with sermons, but with sacrifice.

But in many churches today, discipleship has been reduced to information transfer.

A class.

A curriculum.

A checklist.

Attend six sessions. Memorize a few verses. Graduated with a certificate.

And when life gets messy—when people need more than a sermon—we often retreat.

We retreat because messiness does not fit the schedule.

We retreat because brokenness does not fit the brand.

We retreat because pain requires presence, and presence requires sacrifice.

This is the Great Omission:

- The failure to disciple.
- The failure to walk with people beyond conversion.
- The failure to embody the long obedience in the same direction.

We have taught people how to start the race, but not how to finish it.

We have celebrated decisions, but neglected development.

We have counted baptisms, but not burdens carried.

True discipleship is costly.

It requires time, trust, tears, and tenacity.

It means showing up when it is inconvenient.

It means staying when others walk away.

It means loving when there is no guarantee of return.

Because discipleship is not about producing polished Christians.

It is about forming faithful followers.

Followers who know how to pray in the dark.

How to serve in the storm.

How to love when it hurts.

How to live like Jesus when the world offers every reason not to.

If the Church is to answer the question *"**Where's The Church?**"* with integrity,

It must reclaim discipleship—not as a program, but as a posture.

Not as a product, but as a process.

Not as a task, but as a testimony.

Because when the Church walks with people—Jesus walks with them.

And when Jesus walks with them—***hope is reborn***.

Lisa's Story Revisited

Lisa's story is a tragic example of the *Great Omission*. She was not asking for theological precision—she was asking for presence. She was not seeking doctrinal purity—she was seeking help. She was not questioning the gospel—*she was questioning whether the Church lived it*.

Her church had preached the Great Commission. But when she needed them most, they omitted her. They omitted mercy. They omitted action. They omitted the very heart of Christ.

And in doing so, they answered her question—*"Where's The Church?"*—**_with absence_**.

Reclaiming the Commission

The Church must reclaim the Great Commission—not just as a slogan, but as a lifestyle. We must go. We must discipline. We must teach obedience—not just to theology, but to love.

We must go to the places others avoid.

We must disciple the people others reject.

We must teach the commands others ignore—commands like feeding the hungry, visiting the imprisoned, and loving our enemies.

Because the Great Commission is not just about making converts.

It is about making disciples.

It is about making a difference.

It is about making Jesus visible in a world that has forgotten what He looks like.

Bibliography

1. Holy Bible, English Standard Version. Scriptures cited: Matthew 28:19–20.

2. Bonhoeffer, Dietrich. *The Cost of Discipleship*. SCM Press, 1959.

3. Chan, Francis. *Multiply: Disciples Making Disciples*. David C. Cook, 2012.

4. Wright, N.T. *After You Believe: Why Christian Character Matters*. Harper One, 2010.

5. Stetzer, Ed. "The Great Commission Is Not Optional." Christianity Today, 2015.

6. Barna Group. "State of Discipleship." Barna Research, 2016.

7. Keller, Timothy. *Center Church: Doing Balanced, Gospel-Centered Ministry in Your City*. Zondervan, 2012.

Part II
The Groaning of the World

Chapter 4
The Cry of the Forgotten

Every day, the world groans under the weight of suffering.

Not just in war zones or disaster sites—but in living rooms, shelters, hospitals, and street corners.

The groaning is not poetic —it is visceral.

It is the sound of a mother weeping over an empty pantry.

The silence of a teenager battling depression alone.

The tremble in the voice of a veteran begging for dignity.

The quiet resignation of a refugee clutching a child and a prayer.

These cries rise like incense—holy, aching, desperate.

They ascend from the margins of society, from the shadows of neglect, from the depths of despair.

But unlike incense in the temple, these cries are often unseen.

Unheard.

Unanswered.

They are not distant headlines or abstract statistics.

They are not numbers on a spreadsheet or stories in a documentary.

They are real.

They are near.

They are sacred.

And they are asking one question:

Where is the Church?

Not the building.

Not the brand.

Not the Sunday service.

But the living, breathing Body of Christ.

Where is the Church that feeds the hungry?

That shelters the homeless?

That walks with the grieving?

That defends the oppressed?

Where is the Church that listens without judgment?

That loves without condition?

That serves without hesitation?

Because if the Church is truly the hands and feet of Jesus,

Then the world should feel His touch.

The broken should hear His voice.

The forgotten should know His presence.

But when the Church is silent,

The cries echo louder.

And the question becomes more haunting.

Where is the Church?

This is not a rhetorical question.

It is a summons.

A call to awaken.

A call to respond.

A call to become again what we were always meant to be:

The refuge for the weary.

The voice for the voiceless.

The light in the darkness.

The answer to the cry.

Because when the Church shows up—Jesus shows up.

And when Jesus shows up—*hope is reborn*.

The Faces Behind the Cries

The forgotten are not faceless.

They are not statistics in a report or shadows in the background of society.

They are real.

They are near.

They are sacred.

They are the mothers standing in grocery aisles, calculating whether to buy diapers or dinner.

They are the fathers who quietly skip their medication so their children can have shoes for school.

They are teenagers who smile in public but cry in silence, battling depression with no one to notice.

They are the refugees who have lost everything — home, family, identity—yet still cling to hope as they cross borders and barriers.

They are the seniors who sit alone in nursing homes, forgotten by family, overlooked by society, waiting for someone to remember their name.

They are the veterans who once wore uniforms with honor but now sleep under bridges, invisible to the country they served.

They are the children growing up in homes without heat, without food, without love—learning too early that survival is not guaranteed.

These are the very people Jesus came for.

Not the polished. Not the powerful. Not the popular.

But the poor. The broken. The overlooked. The outcast.

Jesus said,

"Whatever you did for one of the least of these brothers and sisters of mine, you did for me" (Matthew 25:40, NIV).

This was not a metaphor.

It was a **mandate**.

A declaration of how we treat the forgotten is how we treat Him.

That every act of compassion is an act of worship.

That every ignored cry is a missed encounter with Christ Himself.

And yet, when these sacred souls cry out,

The Church is often silent.

Absent.

Indifferent.

We offer prayers but not presence.

We quote Scripture but withhold support.

We build bigger sanctuaries while the streets fill with suffering.

We debate theology while the hungry wait for bread.

This is not the Church Jesus envisioned.

This is not the Body He bled for.

This is not the Bride He is returning for.

Because when the Church turns its back on the least,

It turns its back on the Lord.

When it ignores the cries of the forgotten,

It forgets its own calling.

The forgotten are not a distraction from our mission.

They are the mission.

They are the ones Jesus identified with.

They are the ones He prioritized.

They are the ones He is still waiting for us to see.

Let us be the Church that sees them.

That hears them.

That moves toward them.

That answers their cry not with silence, but with solidarity.

Not with pity, but with presence.

Not with excuses, but with action.

Because when the Church shows up for the forgotten,

Jesus shows up in glory.

And when Jesus shows up—***hope is reborn***.

The Ministry of Presence

Jesus did not ignore the cries of the forgotten.

He did not pass by the broken with polite indifference.

He did not offer distant prayers while withholding His presence.

He moved toward them.

He touched the leper—breaking through the barrier of fear and stigma to restore dignity and healing (Mark 1:41).

He wept with the grieving—entering into their sorrow, not with platitudes, but with tears (John 11:35).

He fed the hungry — refusing to send them away empty, multiplying what little they had into more than enough (Mark 6:42).

He defended the condemned — silencing the stones of judgment and speaking words of mercy to a woman caught in shame (John 8:11).

He listened to the desperate—pausing in a crowd to acknowledge the trembling touch of a woman who had suffered for twelve years (Luke 8:47–48).

His ministry was not just proclamation — it was presence.

It was not just truth — it was tough.

Not just sermons — it was solidarity.

Not just theology — it was tenderness.

Jesus did not wait for people to come to Him clean.

He met them in their mess.

He did not demand perfection before offering compassion.

He brought healing into the very places others avoided.

This is the ministry the Church must recover.

The ministry of presence.

Not just preaching from pulpits but sitting beside hospital beds.

Not just singing worship songs, but walking with the wounded.

Not just quoting Scripture, but living it in the trenches of human suffering.

Not just hosting services, but serving meals.

Not just building platforms, but building relationships.

Presence is powerful.

It does not always have the answers, but it refuses to walk away.

It does not fix everything, but it refuses to ignore anything.

It does not require perfection — it requires proximity.

The Church must become again what Jesus was:

A friend to the outcast.

A companion to the grieving.

A defender of the shamed.

A healer of the broken.

Because the world is not looking for a Church that shouts from a distance.

It is longing for a Church that draws near.

That listens.

That lingers.

That loves.

Let us be that Church.

Let us recover the ministry of presence.

Let us answer the cries of the forgotten not with silence, but with solidarity.

Not with avoidance, but with incarnation.

Not with judgment, but with Jesus.

Because when the Church shows up—Jesus shows up.

And when Jesus shows up—hope is reborn.

When the Church Is Absent

When the Church is absent, the cries of the forgotten do not fade—they echo louder.

They reverberate through empty sanctuaries, through silent pulpits, through unopened doors.

They rise like unanswered prayers, like unfinished songs, like broken promises.

And they ask, again and again, with increasing desperation:

"Where's The Church?"

Lisa's story is a haunting example.

She did not come seeking a sermon — she came seeking support.

She did not need a rebuke — she needed relief.

She did not ask for a building — she longed for belonging.

She did not question God — she questioned whether His people would act like Him.

And when the Church failed to show up, her cry became a lament.

Not just for her own pain, but for the absence of the very body that claimed to carry Christ's heart.

Her final note was not a theological critique—*it was a soul's last plea for mercy*.

It was a mirror held up to the Church, reflecting not its doctrine, but its distance.

This is not just a personal tragedy—it is a prophetic indictment.

It is a warning to every congregation that has confused attendance with action, and purity with presence.

It is a call to repentance for every ministry that has built walls instead of bridges, and budgets instead of benevolence.

Because when the Church fails to respond to suffering,

It fails to reflect Christ.

It fails to embody the One who touched the leper, wept with the grieving, and fed the hungry.

It fails to live out the gospel it proclaims.

When the Church prioritizes programs over people,

It forfeits its witness.

It becomes a performance, not a presence.

A brand, not a body.

A monument, not a movement.

And when the Church ignores the cries of the forgotten,

It becomes irrelevant to the very world it was sent to redeem.

It loses its saltiness.

It dims its light.

It silences its song.

The world is not asking for a perfect Church.

It is pleading for a present one.

A Church that shows up.

That listens.

That loves.

That lingers.

Let Lisa's story not be the end—but the beginning.

Let it be the wake-up call that stirs us from comfort into compassion.

Let it be the lament that leads to revival.

Let it be the question that we finally answer—not with words, but with action.

"Where's The Church?"

Here we are—feeding, healing, walking, weeping, serving, loving. Here we are—reflecting Christ. Here we are—***Rebirthing Hope***.

A Call to Listen and Respond

The Church must learn to listen again.

To hear the cries beneath the silence.

To recognize the sacredness of suffering.

To respond—not with platitudes, but with presence.

Not with judgment, but with justice.

Not with avoidance, but with action.

This is not optional. It is essential.

Because the credibility of the Church is not measured by its theology alone, but by its compassion.

And the world is watching—not to see how well we preach, but how well we love.

Let us be the Church that hears the cry of the forgotten.

That moves toward the margins.

That shows up in the shadows.

That answers the question ***"Where's The Church?"*** with a holy, humble, and healing presence.

Because when the Church shows up—Jesus shows up.

And when Jesus shows up—***Hope is Reborn***.

Bibliography

1. Holy Bible, New International Version. Scriptures cited: Matthew 25:40; Mark 1:41; John 11:35; Mark 6:42; John 8:11; Luke 8:47–48.

2. Bonhoeffer, Dietrich. *The Cost of Discipleship*. SCM Press, 1959.

3. Keller, Timothy. *Ministries of Mercy: The Call of the Jericho Road*. P&R Publishing, 1997.

4. Lupton, Robert D. *Compassion, Justice, and the Christian Life: Rethinking Ministry to the Poor*. Gospel Light, 2007.

5. Nouwen, Henri J.M. *The Wounded Healer: Ministry in Contemporary Society*. Image Books, 1979.

6. Sider, Ronald J. *Rich Christians in an Age of Hunger*. Thomas Nelson, 2005.

7. Barna Group. "The State of Compassion in the Church." Barna Research, 2018.

Chapter 5
The Church in the Shadows

Not every church is absent.

Not every congregation has forgotten the poor, ignored the grieving, or abandoned the broken.

While some have drifted into comfort or compromise, there are others—quiet, faithful, often overlooked—that are ***showing up in the shadows***.

These churches do not make headlines.

They do not trend on social media.

They do not host celebrity pastors or sell-out conferences.

They are not building empires.

But they are building hope.

They are the storefront fellowships that open their doors to the homeless when the shelters are full.

The rural congregations that deliver groceries to widows and single mothers.

The inner-city ministries that tutor children, visit prisons, and walk the streets with prayer and presence.

The immigrant churches that worship in borrowed spaces and serve with borrowed strength.

The house churches that gather in secret yet burn with holy fire.

These churches may not be large, but they are luminous.

They may not be loud, but they are loving.

They may not be famous, but they are faithful.

They are not chasing platforms — they are carrying crosses.

They are not seeking applause — they are sowing mercy.

They are not building brands — they are binding wounds.

They are the ones who show up when no one else does.

Who stays long after the cameras leave.

Who gives without expecting return.

Who serves without seeking recognition.

They are the heartbeat of the gospel.

The hands and feet of Jesus are in forgotten places.

The living answer to the question, ***Where's The Church?***

They are not absent — they are present.

Not in the spotlight, but in the shadows.

Not in the seats of power, but in the trenches of pain.

Not in the echo chambers of comfort, but in the corridors of compassion.

And though the world may not see them, Heaven does.

Though their names may not be known, their faithfulness is recorded in eternity.

Though their work may go unnoticed by men, it is honored by God.

Let us celebrate these churches.

Let us learn from them.

Let us join them.

Because when the Church shows up in the shadows,

Jesus shows up in the light.

And when Jesus shows up—*Hope is Reborn*.

Ministry in the Margins

The Church in the shadows is not defined by its seating capacity, but by its **sending capacity.**

It is not measured by how many gather on Sunday, but by how many are *sent on Monday*.

It is not evaluated by the size of its sanctuary, but by the *scope of its compassion*.

It is not built on visibility—it is built on **voluntary sacrifice**.

It is the storefront congregation that feeds the homeless every Thursday, where folding chairs and paper plates become holy ground.

Where volunteers know names, not just needs.

Where prayer is served alongside soup.

It is the rural fellowship that delivers groceries to widows, driving dusty roads with baskets of bread and arms full of grace.

Where sermons are preached through casseroles and kindness.

Where the gospel arrives in pickup trucks and handwritten notes.

It is the urban ministry that tutors children in underfunded schools,

where pencils and patience become instruments of justice.

Where math problems are solved, and dignity is restored.

Where young minds are told, "***You matter. You are seen. You are loved.***"

It is the prison chaplain who prays with the forgotten,

who walks through locked doors to unlock hearts.

Who listens without judgment.

Who speaks of mercy into places others have abandoned.

It is the pastor who sits beside hospital beds long after visiting hours end,

holding hands, whispering hope, singing hymns in sterile rooms.

Who shows up not for applause, but for presence.

Who carries the weight of grief with sacred tenderness.

These churches are not waiting for recognition.

They are responding to need.

They are not chasing influence.

They are cultivating **impact**.

They are living out Isaiah's call:

"If you spend yourselves on behalf of the hungry and satisfy the needs of the oppressed, then your light will rise in the darkness" (Isaiah 58:10, NIV).

And rise it does.

Not on stages, but in shelters.

Not in spotlights, but in suffering.

Not in fame, but in faithfulness.

Because that is where Jesus is.

Not just in the sanctuary, but in the shadows.

Not just in liturgy, but in the lament.

Not just in the celebration, but in the compassion.

The Church in the shadows is not behind—it is ahead.

It is not weak—it is wise.

It is not forgotten—it is foundational.

It is the answer to the question "***Where's The Church?***"

Not with noise, but with nurture.

Not with spectacle, but with service.

Not with branding, but with brokenness embraced.

And when the Church shows up in the shadows—Jesus shows up in the light.

And when Jesus shows up—***Hope is Reborn***.

Hidden but Holy

The Church in the shadows reflects the ministry of Christ Himself.

Not the Christ of stained-glass grandeur or institutional prestige,

but the Christ who chose obscurity over spectacle, humility over hype, and rejection over recognition.

Jesus was born not in a palace, but in a stable.

Not to applause, but to anonymity.

His arrival was announced to the shepherds, not to the senators.

His cradle was a feeding trough, not a throne.

He lived in humility—walking dusty roads, sharing meals with sinners, and sleeping under open skies.

He did not seek fame—He sought faithfulness.

He did not chase crowds—He called disciples.

He did not build a platform—He built a people.

He healed in homes, not cathedrals.

He taught on hillsides, not in halls of power.

He wept in gardens, not behind pulpits.

He moved through the margins—touching lepers, defending adulterers, dining with tax collectors.

He did not ascend social ladders—He descended into suffering.

And His greatest work was done in the dark.

Not under spotlights, but under the weight of a cross.

Not in celebration, but in crucifixion.

Not in noise, but in silence.

In a borrowed tomb, behind a sealed stone, in the stillness of death—He redeemed the world.

This is the Christ the Church in the shadows reflects.

Not the Christ of celebrity, but the Christ of compassion.

Not the Christ of empire, but the Christ of empathy.

Not the Christ of dominance, but the Christ of descent.

The Church that serves in the shadows is not behind—it is ahead.

It is not weak—it is wise.

It is not forgotten—it is foundational.

It is the Church that chooses presence over platform.

Service over status.

Sacrifice over spotlight.

It is the Church that kneels before it speaks.

That listens before it leads.

That weeps before it worships.

And though it may be hidden from the world, it is honored by Heaven.

Though it may be overlooked by men, it is embraced by God.

Though it may be small in stature, it is mighty in spirit.

Let us not despise the Church in the shadows.

Let us learn from it.

Let us join it.

Let us celebrate it.

Because when the Church reflects the humility of Christ,

It carries the authority of Christ.

And when it serves in the shadows,

It shines with the light of resurrection.

And when Jesus is seen in the shadows—***Hope is Reborn***.

Why We Miss Them

We often overlook these churches because they do not fit our metrics.

They do not have polished branding or celebrity pastors.

They do not host conferences or launch campaigns.

They do not trend on social media or grace the covers of ministry magazines.

They simply serve.

They show up in the silence.

They labor in obscurity.

They give without fanfare.

They love without applause.

And in a culture obsessed with visibility, we forget that God often works invisibly.

We forget that the most powerful movements of the Kingdom are often the least publicized.

That the Spirit moves like wind—felt but unseen (John 3:8).

That the Kingdom grows like yeast—quiet, hidden, transformative (Matthew 13:33).

That the mustard seed becomes a tree not through spectacle, but through surrender (Matthew 13:31–32).

We measure success in numbers.

God measures it in neighborliness.

We chase reach.

God cultivates righteousness.

The Church in the shadows is not failing—it is flourishing.

Not in size, but in sincerity.

Not in the platform, but in the presence.

Not in visibility, but in virtue.

These churches may not be known by the masses,

but they are known by the hungry they feed,

the grieving they comfort,

the children they mentor,

the prisoners they visit,

The widows remember.

They are not building empires—they are building altars.

They are not launching brands—they are lifting burdens.

They are not chasing relevance—they are choosing reverence.

And Heaven sees them.

Heaven honors them.

Heaven records their faithfulness in places no algorithm can reach.

Let us not overlook these churches.

Let us learn from them.

Let us celebrate them.

Let us join them.

Because when the Church flourishes in the shadows,

Jesus is glorified in the light.

And when Jesus is glorified—***Hope is Reborn***.

A Call to Honor

We must learn to honor these churches.

To amplify their stories.

To support their efforts.

To learn from their example.

Because they are answering the question *"**Where's The Church?**"*

Not with marketing—but with mercy.

Not with slogans—but with sacrifice.

Not with noise—but with nurture.

They are the heartbeat of the gospel.

The hands and feet of Jesus.

The light in the darkness.

And when the Church in the shadows shows up—Jesus shows up.
And when Jesus shows up—***Hope is Reborn***.

Bibliography

1. Holy Bible, New International Version. Scriptures cited: Isaiah 58:10; Matthew 13:31–33.

2. Bonhoeffer, Dietrich. *Life Together*. Harper & Row, 1954.

3. Nouwen, Henri J.M. *In the Name of Jesus: Reflections on Christian Leadership*. Crossroad, 1989.

4. Keller, Timothy. *Church in the City: How Urban Ministry Transforms Lives*. Redeemer City to City, 2012.

5. Sider, Ronald J. *The Scandal of the Evangelical Conscience*. Baker Books, 2005.

6. Barna Group. "Small Churches, Big Impact." Barna Research, 2020.

7. Claiborne, Shane. *The Irresistible Revolution: Living as an Ordinary Radical*. Zondervan, 2006.

Chapter 6
When the Church Shows Up

There is a holy power unleashed when the Church shows up.

Not just in word, but in presence.

Not just in belief, but in embodiment.

Not just in buildings, but in broken places.

When the Church shows up, it becomes what it was always meant to be:

Not a monument to memory, but a movement of mercy.

Not a fortress of doctrine, but a field hospital of grace.

Not a spectator of suffering, but a servant in the storm.

When the Church shows up, it carries the weight of heaven into the wounds of earth.

It steps into hospital rooms, prison cells, refugee camps, shelters, classrooms, and street corners.

It does not wait for the hurting to come—it goes to them.

It does not ask for credentials—it responds to need.

It does not measure worthiness—it pours out love.

This is the holy power of presence.

It is the power that turns silence into solidarity.

That turns despair into dignity.

That turns isolation into incarnation.

Because when the Church shows up, it becomes:

- *A living witness*—testifying not just with words, but with wounds healed, tables set, and burdens lifted.
- *A healing body*—binding up the brokenhearted, walking with the weary, and restoring what the world has discarded.
- *A prophetic voice*—speaking truth to power, mercy to judgment, and hope to hopelessness.
- *A visible Christ*—not just remembered in liturgy, but revealed in love.

This is the Church the world is longing for.

Not polished, but present.

Not perfect, but powerful.

Not distant, but divine in its nearness.

Let us be that Church.

Let us show up.

Let us carry the holy power of Christ into the places others avoid.

Let us answer the question *"**Where's The Church?**"* not with rhetoric, but with resurrection.

Because when the Church shows up—Jesus shows up.

And when Jesus shows up—*Hope is Reborn*.

The Power of Presence

When the Church shows up in the hospital room, the grieving are not alone.

The sterile silence is pierced by prayer.

The weight of sorrow is shared.

The presence of compassion becomes a balm for the soul.

When the Church shows up in the shelter, the homeless are not forgotten.

Names are spoken.

Stories are heard.

Dignity is restored in the simple act of sitting, listening, and serving.

When the Church shows up in the prison, the condemned are not beyond reach.

Chains do not define them.

Mistakes do not disqualify them.

The gospel enters through bars and breathes freedom into hearts.

When the Church shows up in the classroom, the overlooked are seen.

Children who have been labeled, ignored, and underestimated suddenly feel known.

Tutors become mentors.

Lessons become lifelines.

And the love of Christ is spelled out in patience and presence.

When the Church shows up in the streets, the voiceless are heard.

Protests become prayers.

Sidewalks become sanctuaries.

The marginalized are no longer invisible—they are embraced.

Because presence is not passive.

It is prophetic.

It is a declaration that says:

"You matter."

"We see you."

"God has not forgotten you."

Presence is the ministry of proximity.

It is the refusal to look away.

It is the courage to enter pain, not just observe it.

It is the embodiment of Emmanuel—God with us.

Jesus modeled this kind of presence.

He did not wait for people to come to Him—He went to them.

He crossed boundaries of culture, class, and comfort.

He broke barriers of religion, reputation, and ritual.

He entered pain—fully, freely, faithfully.

He showed up in the homes of sinners (Luke 19:5–10),

where salvation came not through a sermon, but through a shared meal.

He showed up in the tombs of the possessed (Mark 5:1–20),

where healing came not through distance, but through deliverance.

He showed up in the upper rooms of the fearful (John 20:19),

where peace came not through explanation, but through presence.

And when He showed up—everything changed.

Shame was silenced.

Storms were stilled.

Souls were saved.

Hope was reborn.

This is the power of presence.

This is the ministry of showing up.

This is the calling of the Church.

Let us be the Church that shows up.

In the hospital.

In the shelter.

In the prison.

In the classroom.

In the streets.

Because when the Church shows up—Jesus shows up.

And when Jesus shows up—***Hope is Reborn***.

The Church as Incarnation

The Church is not just called to preach Christ—it is called to embody Him.

To be His hands that heal.

His feet that go.

His voice that comforts.

His heart that breaks for the broken.

We are not merely messengers of the gospel—we are manifestations of it.

We are not just proclaimers of truth—we are participants in grace.

We are not just students of Scripture—we are stewards of presence.

Paul writes,

"Now you are the body of Christ, and each one of you is a part of it" (1 Corinthians 12:27, NIV).

This is not a metaphor—it is a mission.

It is not poetic—it is prophetic.

It is not symbolic—it is sacramental.

We are the visible expression of the invisible God.

We are the continuation of the Incarnation—Christ in us, Christ through us, Christ among us.

We are the presence of Jesus in neighborhoods, nursing homes, and nations.

In shelters and schools.

In prisons and playgrounds.

In boardrooms and back alleys.

When the Church shows up, it becomes a sacrament—an outward sign of inward grace.

It becomes a sanctuary in the storm—a place where the weary find rest, the grieving find comfort, and the broken find healing.

It becomes a table in the wilderness—where bread is broken, stories are shared, and hope is served.

It becomes a light in the darkness—not because it is perfect, but because it is present.

This is the Church the world is longing for.

Not a Church that merely speaks of Jesus, but a Church that looks like Him.

That walks like Him.

That weeps like Him.

That loves like Him.

Because when the Church embodies Christ,

The gospel becomes tangible.

The Kingdom becomes visible.

And hope becomes possible.

Let us be that Church.

Let us carry His heart into the world.

Let us answer the question *"**Where's The Church?**"* not with sermons, but with sacrifice.

Not with programs, but with presence.

Not with noise, but with nurture.

Because when the Church shows up—Jesus shows up.

And when Jesus shows up—***Hope is Reborn***.

The Witness of Action

The world is not waiting for another sermon.

It is not longing for another polished production, another clever series, another theological debate.

It is watching for a Church that lives what it preaches.

A Church whose love is louder than its liturgy.

Whose compassion is deeper than its commentary.

Whose presence is stronger than its platform.

The world is watching for a Church that loves without condition.

That embraces the addict, the outcast, the doubter, the wanderer.

That does not ask for credentials before offering care.

That does not measure worthiness before extending welcome.

It is watching for a Church that serves without a spotlight.

That feeds the hungry without posting it.

That visits the sick without broadcasting it.

That gives quietly, faithfully, sacrificially—because love does not need applause.

It is watching for a Church that gives without expecting return.

That does not barter with blessings.

That does not manipulate with mercy.

That does not tally its generosity but pours it out like oil on the feet of Jesus.

Jesus said,

"Let your light shine before others, that they may see your good deeds and glorify your Father in heaven" (Matthew 5:16, NIV).

This is not a call to performance—it is a call to presence.

To live in such a way that the gospel becomes visible.

Not just in doctrine, but in dinner tables—where strangers become family and bread becomes blessing.

Not just in creeds, but in compassion—where theology is translated into tenderness.

Not just in theology, but in touch—where truth is felt in the embrace of mercy.

This is how the Church regains its credibility.

Not through power, but through presence.

Not through dominance, but through devotion.

Not through control, but through Christlikeness.

Because the world is not asking, ***What do you believe?***

It is asking, ***Do you care?***

It is not asking, "How big is your building?"

It is asking, "How deep is your love?"

It is not asking, "How loud is your worship?"

It is asking, "How real is your witness?"

Let us be the Church that answers with our lives.

Let us shine—not for attention, but for adoration.

Let us serve—not for recognition, but for redemption.

Let us love—not for applause, but for allegiance to Christ.

Because when the Church shows up—not just in word, but in witness—Jesus is seen.

Jesus is known.

Jesus is glorified.

And when Jesus is glorified—***Hope is Reborn***.

Hope Reborn

When the Church shows up, ***hope is reborn***.

Not as a concept, but as a presence.

Not as a theory, but as a touch.

Not as a sermon, but as a shared burden.

Hope is reborn in the eyes of a child who receives a meal—

not just calories, but care.

Not just bread, but belonging.

That child learns that God sees them, and so do we.

Hope is reborn in the heart of a widow who is no longer alone—

when someone knocks, sits, listens, and stays.

When grief is not rushed, and tears are not ignored.

She discovers that love still lingers, and the Church still remembers.

Hope is reborn in the soul of an addict who is finally seen—

not as a problem to fix, but a person to love.

When someone says, "You are more than your struggle."

When grace walks in and shame walks out.

Hope is reborn in the life of a community that is no longer ignored—

when the Church plants gardens in food deserts,

builds bridges across racial divides,

and shows up not just to preach, but to partner.

This is the Church the world is longing for.

Not perfect, but present.

Not polished, but powerful.

Not famous, but faithful.

A Church that does not wait for the world to come to it,

but goes into the world with open hands and open hearts.

A Church that does not hide behind stained glass,

but walks boldly into stained lives.

Let us be that Church.

Let us answer the question *"**Where's The Church?**"*

Not with silence.

Not with slogans.

But with our lives.

Here we are.

In the shadows, where the forgotten dwell.

In the margins, where mercy is needed most.

In the mess, where miracles are born.

In the name of Jesus, who always showed up.

And when the Church shows up—Jesus shows up.

And when Jesus shows up—***Hope is Reborn***.

Bibliography

1. Holy Bible, New International Version. Scriptures cited: Matthew 5:16; Luke 19:5–10; Mark 5:1–20; John 20:19; 1 Corinthians 12:27.

2. Bonhoeffer, Dietrich. *Life Together*. Harper & Row, 1954.

3. Nouwen, Henri J.M. *The Wounded Healer: Ministry in Contemporary Society*. Image Books, 1979.

4. Keller, Timothy. *Generous Justice: How God's Grace Makes Us Just*. Dutton, 2010.

5. Claiborne, Shane. *The Irresistible Revolution: Living as an Ordinary Radical*. Zondervan, 2006.

6. Sider, Ronald J. *Living Like Jesus: Eleven Essentials for Growing a Genuine Faith*. Baker Books, 1996.

7. Barna Group. "Faith in Action: How Churches Are Serving Their Communities." Barna Research, 2021.

Part III

The Call to Rise

Chapter 7
The Church Is Not a Place—It's a People

The question *"Where's The Church?"* is not just a lament—it is a summons.

It is the groan of creation waiting for the sons and daughters of God to be revealed (Romans 8:19).

It is the cry of the wounded, the weary, and the wandering, calling not for explanation, but for incarnation.

It is the ache of a world that has heard sermons but longs to see substance.

It is not just a critique—it is a call.

A call to rise from comfort.

To step beyond the walls of sanctuaries and into the streets of suffering.

To trade performance for presence.

To move from admiration of Christ to imitation of Him.

It is not just a cry for help—it is a commissioning.

A divine invitation to become the answer we've been praying for.

To stop asking God to send someone else, and to say, like Isaiah,

"Here am I. Send me" (Isaiah 6:8, NIV).

Because the Church is not merely called to respond to suffering.

It is called to embody the answer.

To incarnate the gospel.

To enflesh the love of God in real time, in real places, among real people.

To be the hands and feet of Jesus—

Hands that heal, feet that go, hearts that break for what breaks His.

To be the presence of hope in places of despair—

Not just bringing light, but becoming it.

Not just offering peace, but embodying it.

Not just preaching love, but practicing it.

To be the living response to the world's deepest questions:

"Does anyone see me?"

"Does anyone care?"

"Is there still hope?"

"Where is God in all this?"

And the Church must answer—not with platitudes, but with presence.

Not with slogans, but with sacrifice.

Not with silence, but with solidarity.

We are the response.

We are the ones sent.

We are the Church—not a building, but a body.

Not an institution, but an incarnation.

Let us rise to the summons.

Let us heed the call.

Let us embrace the commissioning.

Because when the Church becomes the answer—Jesus becomes visible.

And when Jesus becomes visible—***Hope is Reborn***.

From Observation to Incarnation

Too often, the Church has become a spectator of suffering.

We observe from a distance—safe, sanitized, and removed.

We analyze the pain.

We comment on the crisis.

We offer prayers from afar.

But we do not always enter.

We host panels on poverty, but rarely sit with the poor.

We preach about justice but hesitate to confront injustice.

We sing about healing but avoid the wounded.

We build programs but neglect presence.

We have become comfortable with commentary,

but uncomfortable with compassion.

We have mastered theological precision,

but forgotten relational proximity.

But Jesus did not remain distant.

He did not send sympathy from heaven.

He stepped into the story.

He entered the ache of humanity.

He became flesh and dwelt among us (John 1:14).

He did not just speak truth—He embodied it.

He did not just offer love—He became it.

He touched lepers.

He wept with mourners.

He dined with sinners.

He defended the shamed.

He walked dusty roads, entered broken homes, and carried the weight of our wounds.

Jesus did not spectate—He incarnated.

And if we are to be His Body, we must do the same.

To become the answer, the Church must move from observation to incarnation.

From watching to walking.

From distance to dwelling.

From commentary to compassion.

From programs to presence.

We must stop asking, "*What should be done?*"

And start saying, "*Here we are*."

We must stop waiting for someone else to go.

And start going ourselves.

Because the world is not changed by analysis — it is changed by action.

Not by polished statements, but by sacrificial service.

Not by theological applause, but by incarnational love.

Let us be the Church that enters the story.

That steps into the suffering.

That dwells among the broken.

That becomes the answer.

Because when the Church moves from observation to incarnation—Jesus is seen.

And when Jesus is seen — *Hope is Reborn*.

Building with Broken Stones

The Church is not built with perfect people.

It was never meant to be a gallery of the flawless.

It is not a museum of saints—it is a hospital for sinners.

It is built with broken ones.

With addicts who found grace.

With widows who found family.

With prisoners who found freedom.

With skeptics who found the truth.

With wanderers who found home.

It is built with stories—raw, real, and redeemed.

With scars that testify.

With wounds that have been touched by mercy.

With lives that were once lost and are now living stones.

Peter writes,

"You also, like living stones, are being built into a spiritual house…" (1 Peter 2:5, NIV).

We are not bricks in a monument—we are stones in a movement.

Not uniform, but unique.

Not polished, but placed.

Not perfect, but purposeful.

Each one shaped by mercy—chiseled by grace, refined by fire, softened by love.

Each one placed by grace—not randomly, but intentionally, divinely, beautifully.

Each one is part of the answer—a vital piece in the architecture of hope.

When the Church embraces its brokenness, it becomes a sanctuary for the world's pain.

Not a place that hides wounds, but a place that heals them.

Not a place that denies struggle, but a place that dignifies it.

Not a place that demands perfection, but a place that welcomes imperfection with open arms.

It becomes a mosaic of redemption—a tapestry of testimonies, each shard reflecting the light of Christ.

It becomes a testimony of transformation—a living witness that grace is not just a doctrine, but a destiny.

This is the Church the world needs.

Not a Church that pretends to have it all together,

but a Church that knows it is held together by Jesus.

Not a Church that hides its past,

but a Church that lets its past become a platform for healing.

Let us be that Church.

Let us build with broken stones.

Let us welcome the wounded.

Let us celebrate the redeemed.

Let us become a sanctuary for the world's pain.

Because when the Church embraces its brokenness—Jesus is glorified.

And when Jesus is glorified—***Hope is Reborn***.

Living the Gospel, Not Just Preaching It

The gospel is not just a message to be proclaimed.

It is a life to be lived.

It is not merely a set of doctrines to be defended—it is a divine reality to be demonstrated.

It is not just a truth to be taught—it is a love to be revealed.

It is not confined to pulpits and pages—it is meant to walk the streets, enter homes, and touch wounds.

James reminds us with piercing clarity:

"Faith by itself, if it is not accompanied by action, is dead" (James 2:17, NIV).

Dead faith does not heal.

Dead faith does not feed.

Dead faith does not welcome, defend, or walk beside.

Dead faith may speak—but it does not serve.

To become the answer, the Church must live the gospel in tangible ways.

Not just in Sunday liturgies, but in Monday mercies.

Not just in theological precision, but in relational proximity.

Not just in what we say, but in how we show up.

We must live the gospel by:

- Feeding the hungry—not just with bread, but with dignity.
- Visiting the sick—not just with prayers, but with presence.
- Welcoming the stranger—not just with words, but with warmth and belonging.
- Defending the oppressed—not just with statements, but with solidarity and sacrifice.
- Walking with the wounded—not just with sympathy, but with sustained compassion.

This is not social work—it is spiritual warfare.

It is not a side ministry—it is the main mission.

It is not charity—it is Christianity.

It is not optional—it is obedience.

Because the gospel is not just about going to heaven.

It is about bringing heaven to earth.

It is not just about personal salvation.

It is about communal transformation.

It is not just about what we believe.

It is about how we behave in the name of Jesus.

Let us be the Church that lives the gospel.

That moves from proclamation to incarnation.

From belief to embodiment.

From theory to testimony.

Because when the Church lives the gospel—Jesus is seen.

And when Jesus is seen—*Hope is Reborn*.

A Church on Mission

Becoming the answer means becoming a Church on mission.

Not just a Church with a mission statement, but a Church that lives sent.

Not just sending missionaries overseas, but becoming missionaries in our own neighborhoods.

In apartment complexes and trailer parks.

In coffee shops and classrooms.

In shelters, salons, and street corners.

It means we stop outsourcing compassion.

We stop treating outreach as a department.

We stop waiting for the hurting to come to us—and we go to them.

Not just supporting outreach, but living it.

Not just funding programs, but forming relationships.

Not just hosting events, but holding hands.

Not just inviting people in, but going out—into the margins, into the mess, into the mystery of incarnational love.

Jesus said,

"As the Father has sent me, I am sending you" (John 20:21, NIV).

We stop treating outreach as a department.

We stop waiting for the hurting to come to us—and we go to them.

This is not a suggestion—it is a sending.

This is not a seasonal campaign—it is a lifelong commission.

This is the heartbeat of the Church.

To be sent—not to stay.

To be scattered like seeds—not stored like relics.

To be light in the darkness—not just candles in sanctuaries.

To be salt in the decay—not just seasoning for Sunday sermons.

When the Church embraces its mission, it becomes the answer.

Not just to theological questions, but to human ones:

"Does anyone care?"

"Is there hope for me?"

"Where is God in all this?"

It becomes the answer not just to spiritual needs, but to physical ones:

Hunger.

Loneliness.

Addiction.

Abandonment.

Injustice.

It becomes the answer not just to Sunday services, but to everyday suffering.

In the ER waiting room.

In the foster care system.

In the refugee shelter.

In the funeral procession.

In the broken places where sermons cannot reach—but presence can.

This is the Church the world is longing for.

A Church that moves.

A Church that ministers.

A Church that multiplies mercy.

Let us be that Church.

Let us rise to the sending.

Let us scatter like seeds of hope.

Let us shine like light in the shadows.

Let us preserve like salt in the decay.

Because when the Church embraces its mission—Jesus is revealed.

And when Jesus is revealed—***Hope is Reborn***.

Becoming the Answer

To become the answer is to say:

Here we are.

In the shadows.

In the margins.

In the mess.

In the name of Jesus.

It is to live in such a way that the world no longer asks, ***"Where's the Church?"***

Because the Church is already there.

Already loving.

Already serving.

Already healing.

And when the Church becomes the answer—Jesus becomes visible.
And when Jesus becomes visible—***Hope is Reborn***.

Bibliography

1. Holy Bible, New International Version. Scriptures cited: John 1:14; 1 Peter 2:5; James 2:17; John 20:21.

2. Bonhoeffer, Dietrich. *The Cost of Discipleship*. SCM Press, 1959.

3. Nouwen, Henri J.M. *In the Name of Jesus: Reflections on Christian Leadership*. Crossroad, 1989.

4. Keller, Timothy. *Center Church: Doing Balanced, Gospel-Centered Ministry in Your City*. Zondervan, 2012.

5. Claiborne, Shane. *The Irresistible Revolution: Living as an Ordinary Radical*. Zondervan, 2006.

6. Sider, Ronald J. *Just Generosity: A New Vision for Overcoming Poverty in America*. Baker Books, 2007.

7. Barna Group. "Faithful Presence: How Churches Can Serve Their Communities." Barna Research, 2022.

Chapter 8
The Church We Must Become

The Church is not just a reflection of what has been.

It is a revelation of what could be.

It is not a relic of history—it is a vessel of hope.

Not a monument to memory, but a movement of mercy.

Not a museum of tradition, but a mission of transformation.

The Church is not merely a steward of tradition—it is a steward of transformation.

We honor the past, but we do not idolize it.

We learn from history, but we do not live in it.

We are not called to preserve the past—we are called to proclaim the Kingdom.

To declare that love still heals, grace still saves, and Jesus still reigns.

The world is not waiting for a Church that remembers.

It is longing for a Church that becomes.

Becomes bold—not in arrogance, but in advocacy.

Becomes broken—not in despair, but in dependence.

Becomes beautiful in its obedience—not polished, but powerful in surrender.

We must become the Church that does not retreat from the world's pain,

but runs toward it with open arms and open hearts.

The Church that does not fear the mess,

but enters it with mercy, knowing that Jesus was never afraid of dirt, disease, or despair.

The Church that does not idolize comfort,

but embraces the cross—the place of sacrifice, solidarity, and salvation.

This is the Church the world is aching for.

A Church that bleeds compassion.

A Church that walks into suffering, not away from it.

A Church that trades safety for sacrifice, and relevance for reverence.

Let us become that Church.

Let us rise from the ashes of nostalgia and step into the fire of renewal.

Let us answer the question *"**Where's The Church**?"* not with memory, but with movement.

Not with preservation, but with proclamation.

Not with fear, but with faithfulness.

Because when the Church becomes what it was always meant to be—

Jesus is revealed.

And when Jesus is revealed—***Hope is Reborn***.

A Church That Grows Downward

We often speak of growth in terms of numbers, budgets, and buildings.

We count attendance.

We measure square footage.

We celebrate metrics that impress donors and draw headlines.

But Kingdom growth begins by going downward.

It begins not with elevation, but with humility.

Not with visibility, but with hiddenness.

Not with ambition, but with surrender.

Jesus said,

"Unless a kernel of wheat falls to the ground and dies, it remains only a single seed. But if it dies, it produces many seeds" (John 12:24, NIV).

This is the paradox of the Kingdom:

Life comes through death.

Multiplication comes through surrender.

Impact comes through obscurity.

The Church we must become is not obsessed with visibility, but with fruitfulness.

Not with being seen, but with being faithful.

Not with a platform, but with presence.

Not with applause, but with obedience.

We must become a Church that grows deep, not just wide.

That cultivates roots, not just reach.

That seeks transformation, not just traction.

Because the Kingdom of God is like yeast—quiet, hidden, transformative (Matthew 13:33).

It is like a mustard seed—small, surrendered, yet destined to become shelter (Matthew 13:31–32). It is like a seed that dies—so that others may live.

This is the growth Heaven celebrates:

- A heart laid down in prayer.
- A meal shared with the hungry.
- A burden carried for the broken.
- A life poured out in love.

Let us be the Church that grows downward.

That chooses depth over display.

That chooses surrender over strategy.

That chooses obedience over optics.

Because when the Church dies to self—Christ is revealed.

And when Christ is revealed—***Hope is Reborn***.

A Church That Walks With, Not Just Talks To

The Church we must become does not just preach to the poor—it walks with them.

It does not merely deliver sermons from a distance—it shares meals, stories, and burdens.

It does not reduce poverty to statistics—it sees faces, hears names, and enters homes.

It does not pity—it partners.

It does not patronize—it empowers.

The Church we must become does not just speak about justice—it stands in it.

It does not settle for statements—it shows up in courtrooms, classrooms, and crisis zones.

It does not wait for permission—it moves with conviction.

It does not fear controversy—it fears complicity.

It does not just echo prophetic words—it lives them.

The Church we must become does not just host services—it serves.

It does not measure success by attendance, but by allegiance to Christ.

It does not build bigger buildings while ignoring broken bodies.

It does not entertain—it equips.

It does not perform—it pours out.

Micah reminds us with piercing clarity:

"What does the Lord require of you? To act justly and to love mercy and to walk humbly with your God" (Micah 6:8, NIV).

This is not a suggestion—it is a requirement.

Not a spiritual option, but a sacred obligation.

Not a seasonal campaign, but a lifelong commission.

To walk humbly—not above others, but beside them.

To love mercy—not as a concept, but as a lifestyle.

To act justly—not just in policy, but in proximity.

To walk with the widow—whose grief is sacred and whose story matters.

To walk with the refugee—whose journey is holy and whose dignity must be defended.

To walk with the single mother—whose strength is divine and whose struggle is not invisible.

To walk with the incarcerated father—whose redemption is possible and whose humanity is intact.

To walk with the forgotten elder—whose wisdom is needed and whose presence is precious.

This is the Church the world is longing for.

A Church that walks—not just talks.

A Church that moves—not just meets.

A Church that embodies Micah's mandate—not just memorizes it.

Let us become that Church.

Let us walk into the margins.

Let us walk into the mess.

Let us walk into the mystery of mercy.

Because when the Church walks humbly, loves deeply, and acts justly—
Jesus is seen.

And when Jesus is seen—***Hope is Reborn***.

A Church That Burns With Compassion

The Church we must become is not lukewarm.

It is not content with comfort.

It does not settle for safe.

It does not blend in when it was called to stand out.

It does not whisper when the world needs a prophetic voice.

It is not passive.

It does not wait for permission to love.

It does not delay justice until it is convenient.

It does not outsource compassion or delegate mercy.

It moves. It acts. It shows up.

It is not polite to face injustice.

It does not prioritize reputation over righteousness.

It does not remain neutral when the vulnerable are crushed.

It does not hide behind civility when courage is required.

It speaks truth in love—and love in truth.

It is a Church that burns with holy compassion.

A fire that does not consume, but compels.

A flame that does not destroy, but delivers.

A passion that cannot be quenched by apathy or fear.

It is a Church that weeps over the city as Jesus did (Luke 19:41).

That sees the brokenness and does not look away.

That feels the ache of the streets, the silence of the forgotten, the cry of the oppressed.

That mourns what sin has stolen and longs for what grace can restore.

It is a Church that flips tables when the vulnerable are exploited (Matthew 21:12–13).

That confronts systems of greed and exclusion.

That refuses to let the temple become a marketplace.

That defends the dignity of the poor, the widow, the orphan, the outcast.

It is a Church that lays down its life for the sake of the world (1 John 3:16).

Not just in theory, but in practice.

Not just in martyrdom, but in daily sacrifice.

In giving. In going. In grieving. In grace.

This is not radical—it is biblical.

This is not fringe—it is faithful.

This is not a new idea—it is the ancient path.

The way of the cross.

The way of Christ.

Let us become that Church.

A Church that burns.

A Church that weeps.

A Church that flips tables and carries crosses.

A Church that looks like Jesus—not just in creed, but in courage.

Not just in worship, but in witness.

Because when the Church burns with holy compassion—the world feels the warmth of heaven.

And when the world feels that warmth—***Hope is Reborn***.

A Church That Looks Like Jesus

Ultimately, the Church we must become is the Church that looks like Jesus.

Not just in theology, but in temperament—gentle, truthful, patient, and bold.

Not just in belief, but in behavior—living what we profess, embodying what we proclaim.

Not just in worship, but in witness—carrying the fragrance of Christ into every corner of culture.

Paul writes,

"Follow God's example, therefore, as dearly loved children and walk in the way of love, just as Christ loved us and gave himself up for us…" *(Ephesians 5:1–2, NIV).*

This is not a suggestion—it is a summons.

To follow God's example is to trace the footsteps of Jesus.

To walk in the way of love is to live cruciform—shaped by sacrifice, marked by mercy.

To look like Jesus is to love like Jesus—

With arms wide open.

With no conditions.

With compassion that crosses boundaries and breaks barriers.

To look like Jesus is to serve like Jesus—

Washing feet.

Feeding crowds.

Touching lepers.

Showing up in the places others avoid.

To look like Jesus is to forgive like Jesus—

Even when betrayed.

Even when misunderstood.

Even when the wounds are fresh, and the cost is high.

To look like Jesus is to show up like Jesus—

In homes of sinners.

In tombs of the tormented.

In the upper rooms of the fearful.

In the margins, in the mess, in the mystery of mercy.

This is the Church the world is longing for.

Not a Church of power, but of presence—where people feel seen, known, and loved.

Not a Church of performance, but of proximity—where ministry is measured by nearness, not numbers.

Not a Church of celebrity, but of Christlikeness—where the spotlight fades, and the Savior shines.

The world has seen religion.

It has heard sermons.

It has watched institutions rise and fall.

But it is still asking:

Where is Jesus?

Let us be the Church that answers with our lives.

Let us be the Church that reflects His face, His heart, His hands.

Let us be the Church that walks in the way of love.

Because when the Church looks like Jesus—*Hope is Reborn*.

The Church We Must Become

We must become the Church that:

- **Laments** with the broken.
- **Listens** before it lectures.
- **Leads** with love, not fear.
- **Lifts** the lowly.
- **Lives** the gospel, not just preaches it.

We must become the Church that answers the question "Where's The Church?"

Not with branding, but with **burden-bearing**.

Not with slogans, but with **sacrifice**.

Not with silence, but with **solidarity**.

Because when the Church becomes what it was always meant to be—
Jesus is revealed.

And when Jesus is revealed—***Hope is Reborn.***

Bibliography

1. Holy Bible, New International Version. Scriptures cited: John 12:24; Micah 6:8; Luke 19:41; Matthew 21:12–13; 1 John 3:16; Ephesians 5:1–2.
2. Bonhoeffer, Dietrich. *The Cost of Discipleship*. SCM Press, 1959.
3. Nouwen, Henri J.M. *Compassion: A Reflection on the Christian Life*. Image Books, 1982.
4. Keller, Timothy. *Ministries of Mercy: The Call of the Jericho Road*. P&R Publishing, 1997.
5. Claiborne, Shane. *The Irresistible Revolution: Living as an Ordinary Radical*. Zondervan, 2006.
6. Tisby, Jemar. *The Color of Compromise: The Truth about the American Church's Complicity in Racism*. Zondervan, 2019.
7. Barna Group. "The State of the Church: What Americans Believe." Barna Research, 2023.

Chapter 9
Hope Is Reborn

Hope is not a sentiment—it is a substance.

It is not a fleeting feeling stirred by circumstance.

It is not a shallow cheerfulness that ignores pain.

It is the deep-rooted assurance that even in the valley of death, life is rising.

Hope is the soil in which resurrection takes root.

It is the breath of God in the lungs of the weary.

It is the anchor that holds when everything else breaks loose.

Hope is not a wish—it is a witness.

It testifies to what God has done, and what He will do again.

It stands in the rubble and declares, "This is not the end."

It looks at the tomb and sees a garden.

It looks at the cross and sees a crown.

Hope is not passive—it is prophetic.

It does not deny reality—it defines it with resurrection truth.

Hope is not a vague optimism—it is a resurrection reality.

It is grounded in the empty grave.

It is sealed by the scars of Christ.

It is fueled by the Spirit who raised Jesus from the dead (Romans 8:11).

It is not wishful thinking—it is Kingdom certainty.

It is not naïve—it is anchored in eternity.

And when the Church shows up—hope is reborn.

Not because the Church is perfect, but because Christ is present.

Not because we have all the answers, but because we embody the Answer.

Not because we are strong, but because we are surrendered.

Hope is reborn in the eyes of the hungry child who receives a meal.

In the heart of the grieving widow who is no longer alone.

In the soul of the addict who is finally seen.

In the life of the community, that is no longer ignored.

Hope is reborn when the Church stops hiding and starts healing.

When we stop performing and start participating.

When we stop preserving our comfort and start pursuing the cross.

Let us be that Church.

Let us carry that hope.

Let us show up—not with perfection, but with presence.

Not with answers, but with availability.

Not with strength, but with surrender.

Because when the Church shows up—Jesus shows up.

And when Jesus shows up—*Hope is Reborn*.

Hope in the Shadows

Hope is reborn in the shadows, where light is most needed.

Not in the spotlight of platforms, but in the quiet corners of pain.

Not in the applause of crowds, but in the ache of the overlooked.

Hope does not rise in sanitized sanctuaries—it rises in sacred suffering.

Hope is reborn in hospital rooms, where grief hangs heavy.

Where diagnoses shatter dreams.

Where families whisper prayers between beeping monitors.

Where tears fall on sterile floors and faith clings to fragile breath.

The Church must not pass by these rooms—it must enter them with tenderness and truth.

Hope is reborn in shelters, where dignity has been stripped.

Where names are forgotten, and stories are dismissed.

Where survival replaces celebration.

Where the warmth of a blanket and the kindness of a meal become holy acts of restoration.

The Church must not pity from afar—it must sit, listen, and serve.

Hope is reborn in prisons, where shame has settled.

Where chains are not just physical, but emotional and spiritual.

Where regret echoes through concrete walls.

Where redemption is still possible, and grace still reaches.

The Church must not condemn—it must proclaim freedom to the captives (Luke 4:18).

Hope is reborn in classrooms, where potential has been overlooked.

Where children carry burdens too heavy for their age.

Where dreams are dismissed because of zip codes or skin color.

Where a word of affirmation can ignite a future.

The Church must not ignore these spaces—it must invest in, uplift, and advocate for them.

Hope is reborn in streets, where voices have been silenced.

Where injustice walks freely.

Where systems fail and suffering multiplies.

Where protests cry out for dignity and peace.

The Church must not remain neutral—it must walk in solidarity and speak with courage.

The Church does not bring hope by avoiding these places.

It brings hope by entering them.

By showing up—not just once, but consistently.

By staying—not just for photo ops, but for transformation.

By serving—not to be seen, but to see others.

Jesus said,

"You are the light of the world... let your light shine before others, that they may see your good deeds and glorify your Father in heaven" *(Matthew 5:14, 16, NIV).*

Light does not shine in theory—it shines in proximity.

It shines when we move toward the pain.

When we step into the shadows.

When we carry candles into caves of despair.

Hope is not reborn by programs—it is reborn by presence.

By the ministry of showing up.

By the power of proximity.

By the witness of love that lingers.

Let us be that Church.

Let us bring light to where it is most needed.

Let us enter the shadows—not with fear, but with faith.

Because when the Church shows up—Jesus shows up.

And when Jesus shows up—***Hope is Reborn***.

Hope in the Margins

Hope is reborn in the margins, where society forgets but God remembers.

Where systems overlook, but heaven leans in.

Where power turns away, but love draws near.

The margins are not empty—they are sacred.

They are not abandoned—they are anointed.

Hope is reborn where the widow waits—

in silence, in sorrow, in sacred longing.

She is not invisible to God.

She is not forgotten by the Kingdom.

She is the heartbeat of divine compassion (James 1:27).

Hope is reborn where the refugee flees—

carrying trauma, crossing borders, searching for safety.

The Church must not build walls—it must open doors.

Not just with shelter, but with solidarity.

Not just with aid, but with honor.

Hope is reborn where the single mother struggles—

juggling work, children, and exhaustion.

She is not a statistic—she is a story.

She is not a burden—she is beloved.

The Church must not offer pity—it must offer partnership.

Hope is reborn where the elder is overlooked—

in nursing homes, in quiet apartments, in forgotten corners.

Their wisdom is not expired.

Their presence is not peripheral.

The Church must not discard—it must dignify.

The Church must not be a fortress—guarded, gated, and distant.

It must be a field hospital—mobile, messy, and merciful.

A place where wounds are tended, not judged.

Where stories are honored, not edited.

Where mercy is multiplied, not rationed.

Paul writes,

"God chose the lowly things of this world and the despised things… to nullify the things that are" (1 Corinthians 1:28, NIV).

This is the upside-down Kingdom.

Where the last are first.

Where the broken are blessed.

Where the margins become the miracle site.

Not the stage.

Not the spotlight.

But the sidewalk.

The shelter.

The silence.

Let us be the Church that lives in the margins.

That listens before it lectures.

That lingers before it leaves.

That loves before it labels.

Because when the Church enters the margins—Jesus is revealed.

And when Jesus is revealed—***Hope is Reborn***.

Hope in the Mess

Hope is reborn in the mess, not in sanitized sanctuaries.

Not in polished programs or pristine pews.

Not in curated worship sets or choreographed services.

Hope rises in the raw places.

In the unfiltered, unedited, unguarded spaces where pain is real, and presence is rare.

Hope is reborn in addiction recovery circles—

where stories are jagged,

where shame is thick,

where grace is the only glue holding lives together.

Where relapse is met with compassion,

and every step toward healing is celebrated as sacred ground.

Hope is reborn in foster care visits—

where children carry trauma in their eyes,

and caseworkers carry burdens in their hearts.

Where the Church must not just donate toys,

but offer time, trust, and tenderness.

Where love must be patient, persistent, and proximate.

Hope is reborn in late-night phone calls—

when someone says, "I don't know if I can make it,"

and the Church does not respond with a voicemail,

but with a voice.

With presence.

With prayer.

With the ministry of staying awake when others sleep.

Hope is reborn in food pantry lines—

where dignity is often the hungriest need.

Where the Church must not just hand out groceries,

but hand out grace.

Where names are remembered,

stories are honored,

and every bag of rice becomes a testimony of provision.

Jesus did not avoid the mess—He entered it.

He touched lepers—breaking social taboos to restore human touch.

He dined with sinners—sharing tables before sharing theology.

He walked through Samaria—crossing cultural boundaries to meet a woman at a well.

He knelt in Gethsemane—sweating blood, bearing sorrow, embracing agony.

To follow Him is to follow Him into the mess.

Not with judgment, but with joy—the kind that dances in the dark.

Not with fear, but with faith—the kind that walks on water and weeps with the broken.

Not with distance, but with incarnational love—the kind that moves in, stays close, and never lets go.

This is the Church the world is longing for.

A Church that does not flinch at brokenness.

A Church that does not sanitize suffering.

A Church that does not retreat from reality.

Let us be that Church.

Let us enter the mess—not to fix, but to fellowship.

Not to control, but to carry.

Not to escape, but to embrace.

Because when the Church enters the mess—Jesus is revealed.

And when Jesus is revealed—***Hope is Reborn***.

Hope in the Name of Jesus

Hope is reborn in the **name of Jesus**.

Not in our branding, but in our **burden-bearing**.

Not in our eloquence, but in our **obedience**.

Not in our buildings, but in our **becoming**.

Peter declared,

"Salvation is found in no one else… for there is no other name under heaven… by which we must be saved" (Acts 4:12, NIV).

This is the name we carry.

This is the name we serve.

This is the name we embody.

When the Church shows up in the name of Jesus—***Hope is Reborn***.

In the eyes of a child who receives a meal.

In the heart of a widow who is no longer alone.

In the soul of an addict who is finally seen.

In the life of a community that is no longer ignored.

This is the Church the world is longing for.

Not perfect, but present.

Not polished, but powerful.

Not famous, but faithful.

Let us be that Church.

Let us answer the question *"**Where's The Church?**"*

Not with silence.

Not with slogans.

But with our **lives**.

Here we are.

In the shadows.

In the margins.

In the mess.

In the name of Jesus.

And when the Church shows up—**Jesus shows up**.

And when Jesus shows up—***Hope is Reborn**.*

Bibliography

1. Holy Bible, New International Version. Scriptures cited: Matthew 5:14, 16; 1 Corinthians 1:28; Acts 4:12.

2. Bonhoeffer, Dietrich. *Life Together*. Harper & Row, 1954.

3. Nouwen, Henri J.M. *The Wounded Healer: Ministry in Contemporary Society*. Image Books, 1979.

4. Keller, Timothy. *Hope in Times of Fear: The Resurrection and the Meaning of Easter*. Viking, 2021.

5. Claiborne, Shane. *Jesus for President: Politics for Ordinary Radicals*. Zondervan, 2008.

6. Tisby, Jemar. *How to Fight Racism: Courageous Christianity and the Journey Toward Racial Justice*. Zondervan, 2021.

7. Barna Group. "Faith in Action: How Churches Can Be a Catalyst for Community Renewal." Barna Research, 2023.

Part IV

Rebuilding the Church That Jesus Imagined

Chapter 10
Blueprint of a Living Church

The question *"Where's The Church?"* echoes across generations, across neighborhoods, across nations.

It is not a new question—it is an ancient cry.

It rises from the rubble of war zones and the silence of segregated pews.

It is whispered in hospital corridors and shouted in protest marches.

It is etched into the eyes of the abandoned, the abused, the overlooked.

It is asked in the aftermath of tragedy—

when the headlines fade but the pain remains.

When the world watches and wonders:

Will the Church show up, or stay silent?

It is asked in the silence of injustice—

when systems fail and the vulnerable fall through the cracks.

When the oppressed cry out and the powerful look away.

When justice is delayed, denied, or distorted.

It is asked in the ache of abandonment—

when the widow sits alone.

When the foster child waits for a home.

When the addict relapses, and no one answers the phone.

When the elder is forgotten in a room full of memories.

This is not a question of geography—it is a question of presence.

Not "Where is your building?" but "Where is your body?"

Not "Where do you gather?" but "Where do you go?"

Not "What do you believe?" but "Whom do you become?"

And the answer must be more than words.

More than branding.

More than well-meaning intentions.

The world is not waiting for another mission statement.

It is waiting for a movement of mercy.

A people who don't just talk about Jesus—but look like Him.

The answer must be embodied.

It must be lived.

It must be felt in the margins,

Heard in the silence,

Seen in the shadows.

The Church must rise and say, with humility and conviction:

Here we are.

Here we are—in the mess.

Here we are—in the margins.

Here we are—in the mourning.

Here we are—not with all the answers, but with open arms.

Not with perfection, but with presence.

Not with fear, but with faith.

Because when the Church shows up—Jesus shows up.

And when Jesus shows up—***Hope is Reborn***.

Here We Are—in the Shadows

We are not afraid of the dark.

We do not flinch when the shadows fall.

We do not retreat when the night grows long.

Because we know that darkness is not the absence of God—it is the invitation for light.

We are not called to curse the darkness—we are called to carry the flame.

We do not flee from pain.

We do not sanitize suffering or sidestep sorrow.

We do not offer platitudes when presence is required.

We enter the ache.

We sit in the silence.

We hold space for lament, knowing that tears are sacred and healing begins with proximity.

We do not hide from grief.

We do not rush the process or avoid the weight.

We walk with the grieving through the valley of the shadow.

We show up—not with answers, but with arms.

Not with solutions, but with solidarity.

We show up in hospital rooms,

where monitors beep, and prayers are whispered.

Where diagnoses are delivered, and hope feels fragile.

Where the presence of the Church becomes the presence of Christ.

We show up in funeral homes,

where memories are held like fragile glass.

Where families gather in mourning and mystery.

Where the Church becomes a voice of resurrection in the valley of death.

We show up in late-night crises,

when the phone rings at 2 a.m.

When someone says, "I don't know if I can make it."

When despair knocks, and the Church answers—not with fear, but with faith.

We show up in places where hope flickers and faith feels fragile.

Where the light is dim but not extinguished.

Where the embers of belief need breath.

Where the Church becomes the wind of the Spirit, fanning flames back to life.

Because Jesus said,

"I am the light of the world. Whoever follows me will never walk in darkness..." (John 8:12, NIV).

And if He is the light, then we must carry it.

Not to the spotlight, but to the shadows.

Not to the stage, but to the suffering.

Not to the places of applause, but to the places of agony.

Not to the platforms of prestige, but to the people in pain.

This is the Church the world is longing for.

A Church that shines—not for attention, but for healing.

A Church that glows—not with performance, but with presence.

A Church that walks into the dark—not to escape it, but to transform it.

Let us be that Church.

Let us carry the light.

Let us show up in the night.

Because when the Church enters the darkness—Jesus is revealed.

And when Jesus is revealed—***Hope is Reborn***.

Here We Are—in the Margins

We are not called to the center of power.

We are not called to climb ladders of influence or chase seats at elite tables.

We are not called to mirror the empires of this world.

We are called to descend—to stoop low, to serve deep, to love wide.

Because the Gospel does not ascend to dominate—it descends to deliver.

We are called to the edges of compassion.

To the places where maps fade, and headlines move on.

To the margins where pain lingers and hope is scarce.

To the forgotten fields where no one else is looking—

but where God is already waiting.

We are called to the places where society forgets, but God remembers.

Where the world sees waste, God sees worth.

Where the world sees problems, God sees people.

Where the world sees margins, God sees miracle sites.

We walk with the widow—

not just in sympathy, but in solidarity.

We carry her grief, honor her story, and remind her she is not alone.

Because pure religion is not performance—it is presence (James 1:27).

We welcome the refugee—

not as a stranger, but as a sibling.

We open our doors, our tables, our hearts.

Because hospitality is not a program—it is a posture.

And Jesus Himself was once a refugee (Matthew 2:13–15).

We stand with the single mother—

not with pity, but with partnership.

We affirm her strength, support her journey, and surround her with community.

Because the Church is not a place of shame—it is a place of shelter.

We honor the elder—

not by placing them on the shelf, but by placing them at the center.

We listen to their wisdom.

We learn from their scars.

We remember that longevity is not a liability—it is a legacy.

Paul reminds us,

"God chose the lowly things of this world and the despised things—and the things that are not—to nullify the things that are" (1 Corinthians 1:28, NIV).

This is the upside-down Kingdom.

Where the last are first.

Where the broken are blessed.

Where the poor are rich in faith (James 2:5).

Where the margins become the miracle site.

Not the palace, but the prison.

Not the temple, but the tomb.

Not the throne room, but the manger.

This is where Jesus shows up.

And if we are to be His Body, this is where we must go.

Let us be the Church that walks the edges.

That listens before it leads.

That kneels before it speaks.

That loves without condition and serves without applause.

Because when the Church moves to the margins—Jesus is revealed.

And when Jesus is revealed—***Hope is Reborn***.

Here We Are—in the Mess

We do not sanitize suffering.

We do not edit pain to make it palatable.

We do not wrap grief in platitudes or hide brokenness behind stained glass.

We do not pretend that faith erases struggle—

we proclaim that faith enters it.

Because the Gospel is not afraid of blood, sweat, or tears.

It was born in a manger, baptized in a river, and crowned on a cross.

We do not curate compassion.

We do not serve only when it is convenient.

We do not love only when it is clean.

We do not filter mercy through metrics or manage kindness through committees.

We do not wait for the perfect moment—

we move in the present mess.

We do not avoid the uncomfortable.

We do not flinch at addiction.

We do not look away from trauma.

We do not silence lament or rush healing.

We believe that sacred ground is often found in the most shattered places.

So we enter addiction recovery circles—

not as experts, but as companions.

We listen without judgment.

We celebrate every step toward freedom.

We believe that sobriety is not just possible—it is holy.

We visit foster homes—

not just to drop off donations, but to drop into lives.

We advocate for children.

We support weary caseworkers.

We remind every child that they are seen, known, and loved.

We answer late-night calls—

when despair whispers lies and hope feels out of reach.

We do not send it to voicemail.

We show up.

We stay.

We speak life into the silence.

We serve in food pantry lines—

not as saviors, but as servants.

We hand out groceries with dignity.

We learn names.

We hear stories.

We remember that Jesus said, "I was hungry, and you gave me something to eat" (Matthew 25:35, NIV).

Jesus did not avoid the mess—He entered it.

He touched lepers—breaking social taboos to restore human touch.

He dined with sinners—sharing tables before sharing theology.

He walked through Samaria—crossing cultural boundaries to meet the outcast.

He knelt in Gethsemane—sweating blood, bearing sorrow, embracing agony.

To follow Him is to follow Him into the mess.

Not with judgment, but with joy—the kind that dances in the dark.

Not with fear, but with faith—the kind that walks on water and weeps with the broken.

Not with distance, but with incarnational love—the kind that moves in, stays close, and never lets go.

This is the Church the world is longing for.

A Church that does not flinch at brokenness.

A Church that does not sanitize suffering.

A Church that does not retreat from reality.

Let us be that Church.

Let us enter the mess—not to fix, but to fellowship.

Not to control, but to carry.

Not to escape, but to embrace.

Because when the Church enters the mess—Jesus is revealed.

And when Jesus is revealed—***Hope is Reborn***.

Here We Are—in the Name of Jesus

We do not show up in our own strength.

We do not serve in our own name.

We do not love with our own capacity.

We show up in the name of Jesus.

The name that heals.

The name that restores.

The name that saves.

Peter declared,

"Salvation is found in no one else… for there is no other name under heaven… by which we must be saved" (Acts 4:12, NIV).

This is the name we carry.

This is the name we embody.

This is the name we proclaim—not just with words, but with **witness**.

Here We Are—Together

We are not solo saviors.

We are not isolated saints.

We are a body.

A movement.

A mosaic of mercy.

We are the Church.

Not perfect, but present.

Not polished, but powerful.

Not famous, but faithful.

We answer the question *"**Where's The Church?**"*

Not with silence.

Not with slogans.

But with our **lives**.

Here we are.

In the shadows.

In the margins.

In the mess.

In the name of Jesus.

And when the Church shows up—**Jesus shows up**.

And when Jesus shows up—***Hope is Reborn***.

Bibliography

1. Holy Bible, New International Version. Scriptures cited: John 8:12; 1 Corinthians 1:28; Acts 4:12.

2. Bonhoeffer, Dietrich. *Life Together*. Harper & Row, 1954.

3. Nouwen, Henri J.M. *The Wounded Healer: Ministry in Contemporary Society*. Image Books, 1979.

4. Keller, Timothy. *Generous Justice: How God's Grace Makes Us Just*. Dutton, 2010.

5. Claiborne, Shane. *The Irresistible Revolution: Living as an Ordinary Radical*. Zondervan, 2006.

6. Tisby, Jemar. *How to Fight Racism: Courageous Christianity and the Journey Toward Racial Justice*. Zondervan, 2021.

7. Barna Group. "Faith in Action: How Churches Can Be a Catalyst for Community Renewal." Barna Research, 2023.

Chapter 11
The Ministry of Showing Up

The most powerful ministry is not always preached—it is present.

It does not require a microphone or a stage.

It does not depend on eloquence or applause.

It happens in living rooms, hospital corridors, and street corners.

It happens when someone says, "I'm here," and means it.

It happens when love refuses to leave.

It is not always eloquent—it is embodied.

It is not polished—it is personal.

It is not scripted—it is sincere.

It is the ministry of eye contact, of shared tears, of quiet prayers.

It is the Gospel with skin on.

It is Christ in us, moving toward the pain.

It is not always planned—it is proximate.

It interrupts our schedules.

It disrupts our comfort.

It calls us to be available, not just organized.

To be interruptible, not just efficient.

To be near, not just aware.

In a world of noise, presence speaks louder than words.

In a culture of performance, presence breaks through with authenticity.

In a Church tempted by spectacle, presence returns us to the simplicity of incarnational love.

This is the ministry of showing up.

Not with perfection, but with presence.

Not with answers, but with availability.

Not with credentials, but with compassion.

It is the ministry of the Samaritan who crossed the road (Luke 10:33).

The ministry of Mary, who stayed at Jesus' feet (Luke 10:39).

The ministry of Jesus, who wept with the grieving (John 11:35).

The ministry of the early Church, which broke bread daily and shared everything they had (Acts 2:44–46).

This ministry does not require a seminary degree.

It requires a surrendered heart.

It does not demand charisma.

It demands courage.

To show up is to say:

"I see you."

"I hear you."

"I will not leave you."

Let us be that Church.

Let us reclaim the ministry of showing up.

Let us move toward the margins, the mess, the mourning.

Let us carry the presence of Christ—not just in our preaching, but in our proximity.

Because when the Church shows up—Jesus is revealed.

And when Jesus is revealed—***Hope is Reborn***.

Showing Up in the Ordinary

The ministry of showing up begins in the ordinary.

Not in the spotlight, but in the shadows.

Not in the headlines, but in the hidden places.

Not in the grand gestures, but in the quiet consistencies that whisper, "You are not alone."

It begins in the daily, the mundane, the overlooked.

In the routines that seem small but carry eternal weight.

In the unnoticed moments that heaven sees and honors.

It is the phone call returned—

not because we have the right words,

but because presence matters more than perfection.

Because sometimes the sound of a familiar voice is enough to steady a soul.

It is the meal delivered—

not gourmet, but grace-filled.

A casserole becomes communion.

A warm plate becomes a reminder: ***"You are seen. You are loved."***

It is the ride offered—

to the doctor's office, the job interview, the shelter.

It is the ministry of movement—of going the extra mile,

of turning a car into a sanctuary of kindness.

It is the prayer whispered in a hallway—

not shouted from a stage,

but spoken in trembling faith.

A hand on a shoulder. A tear shared.

A moment that heaven records.

Jesus showed up in the ordinary.

In homes where mothers wept, and children played.

In boats, calming storms, and calling disciples.

In fields, feeding the hungry and teaching the crowds.

In funerals, where He wept before He resurrected.

He did not wait for a pulpit—He made the world His platform.

He did not wait for a crowd—He moved toward the one.

The bleeding woman.

The tax collector in a tree.

The man by the pool.

The child on His lap.

Paul reminds us,

"Rejoice with those who rejoice; mourn with those who mourn"
(Romans 12:15, NIV)

This is not a strategy—it is a sacrifice.

To enter someone's joy without envy.

To carry someone's grief without rushing it.

To be present in someone's pain without needing to fix it.

This is the ministry of showing up.

It is not glamorous, but it is glorious.

It is not efficient, but it is eternal.

It is not always noticed, but it is never wasted.

Let us be the Church that shows up in the ordinary.

That honors the mundane.

That believes every moment can be holy.

Because when we show up in the ordinary—Jesus is revealed.

And when Jesus is revealed—***Hope is Reborn***.

Showing Up in the Broken Places

The ministry of showing up is most needed in the broken places.

Not in the spotlight, but in the shadows.

Not in the sanctuary, but in the storm.

Not where things are polished, but where people are in pieces.

It is needed in the ER waiting room—

where families sit in silence,

where diagnoses hang heavy in the air,

where the presence of a friend becomes the presence of Christ.

Here, ministry is not a sermon—it is a seat beside the suffering.

It is needed in the courtroom—

where justice is weighed, and lives are changed.

Where fear walks in with every defendant.

Where the Church must not just pray for justice,

but stand beside those who feel condemned,

offering grace, advocacy, and a reminder of dignity.

It is needed in the shelter—

where stories of trauma echo through cinderblock walls.

Where children sleep in unfamiliar beds.

Where mothers carry more than bags—they carry burdens.

Here, ministry is not a program—it is a presence that says, ***"You are not forgotten."***

It is needed in the prison—

where shame has settled, and hope feels distant.

Where the Church must not just preach freedom,

but embody it—through letters, visits, and the radical belief

that redemption is possible even behind bars.

It is not glamorous.

There are no lights, no applause, no curated moments.

Just raw humanity.

Just sacred suffering.

Just the holy ground of brokenness.

It is not easy.

It costs time.

It costs comfort.

It costs control.

But it is the cost of compassion.

But it is holy.

Because Jesus showed up in the broken places.

He touched lepers—breaking social barriers to restore human dignity (Mark 1:41).

He wept at Lazarus's tomb—entering grief before offering resurrection (John 11:35).

He stood beside the woman caught in adultery—defending her dignity before declaring her freedom (John 8:10–11).

He walked through Samaria—crossing cultural divides to meet a woman in her shame and offer living water (John 4:4–26).

To follow Him is to follow Him into the brokenness.

Not to fix it, but to fellowship in it.

Not to control it, but to carry it.

Not to escape it, but to embrace it.

This is the Church the world is longing for.

A Church that does not flinch at pain.

A Church that does not sanitize suffering.

A Church that does not retreat from reality.

Let us be that Church.

Let us show up in the broken places.

Let us kneel beside the hurting.

Let us walk into the mess with mercy.

Let us carry the light of Christ—not to condemn, but to commune.

Because when the Church enters the brokenness—Jesus is revealed.

And when Jesus is revealed—***Hope is Reborn***.

Showing Up in the Name of Jesus

The ministry of showing up is not powered by personality—it is powered by presence.

Not charisma, but compassion.

Not performance, but proximity.

Not the strength of our voice, but the surrender of our hearts.

It is not about being impressive—it is about being available.

And this presence is not our own—it is Christ's.

We do not show up in our own name.

We do not serve in our own strength.

We do not love with our own capacity.

We show up in the name of Jesus.

The name that heals—

not just bodies, but memories.

Not just wounds, but identities.

Not just sickness, but shame.

The name that restores—

families torn apart.

Dreams deferred.

Hope buried beneath years of silence.

The name that saves—

from sin, from despair, from isolation.

The name that breaks chains and builds bridges.

The name that turns tombs into testimonies.

Peter declared,

"Silver or gold I do not have, but what I do have I give you. In the name of Jesus Christ... walk" (Acts 3:6, NIV).

This is the power of presence.

Not wealth.

Not influence.

Not credentials.

We may not have silver or gold.

We may not have platforms or prestige.

But we have presence.

We have the Spirit.

We have the name of Jesus.

And when we show up in His name—***Hope is Reborn***.

Not because we are enough, but because He is.

Not because we are strong, but because He is near.

Not because we are worthy, but because He is willing.

This is the ministry the world is longing for.

A Church that does not rely on personality, but on presence.

A Church that does not chase applause, but carries anointing.

A Church that does not just speak the name of Jesus, but embodies it.

Let us be that Church.

Let us show up in His name.

Let us walk into broken places with healing in our hands.

Let us speak into silence with resurrection in our voice.

Let us carry the name of Jesus—not as a slogan, but as a sacred summons.

Because when the Church shows up in His name—Jesus is revealed.

And when Jesus is revealed—***Hope is Reborn***.

Showing Up Together

The ministry of showing up is not a solo act—it is a **shared calling**.

We show up together.

As a body.

As a family.

As a movement of mercy.

We show up in worship.

We show up in outreach.

We show up in advocacy.

We show up in lament.

Because the Church is not a building—it is a **body**.

Not a place to attend, but people who **ascend** into the broken places with love.

Let us be that Church.

Let us show up.

Let us answer the question *"**Where's The Church?**"*

Not with silence.

Not with slogans.

But with our **lives**.

Here we are.

In the ordinary.

In the broken.

In the name of Jesus.

Together.

And when the Church shows up—**Jesus is revealed**.

And when Jesus is revealed—***Hope is Reborn***.

Bibliography

1. Holy Bible, New International Version. Scriptures cited: Romans 12:15; Mark 1:41; John 11:35; John 8:10–11; John 4:4–26; Acts 3:6.

2. Bonhoeffer, Dietrich. *Life Together*. Harper & Row, 1954.

3. Nouwen, Henri J.M. *The Wounded Healer: Ministry in Contemporary Society*. Image Books, 1979.

4. Keller, Timothy. *Ministries of Mercy: The Call of the Jericho Road*. P&R Publishing, 1997.

5. Claiborne, Shane. *The Irresistible Revolution: Living as an Ordinary Radical*. Zondervan, 2006.

6. Tisby, Jemar. *How to Fight Racism: Courageous Christianity and the Journey Toward Racial Justice*. Zondervan, 2021.

7. Barna Group. "Faith in Action: How Churches Can Be a Catalyst for Community Renewal." Barna Research, 2023.

Chapter 12
The Power of Proximity

Proximity is not just geography—it is ministry.

It is not measured in miles, but in mercy.

It is not about being in the same room—it is about being in the same reality.

Proximity is the sacred decision to move toward someone, not just physically, but spiritually, emotionally, and relationally.

It is the refusal to remain detached.

It is the courage to be with.

It is not about being nearby—it is about being with.

Within the pain.

Within the process.

Within the questions that have no easy answers.

Proximity says, "I won't leave you alone in this."

It is the ministry of presence, not performance.

It is not about physical closeness alone—it is about spiritual nearness, emotional availability, and relational presence.

It is the kind of nearness that listens without rushing.

That stays without fixing.

That loves without condition.

It is the kind of presence that says, "I see you. I hear you. I am here."

In a world of distance, proximity is radical.

Where screens separate and schedules isolate, proximity breaks through with embodied compassion.

It defies the cultural drift toward disconnection.

It chooses inconvenience for the sake of intimacy.

In a culture of isolation, proximity is healing.

It restores dignity.

It rebuilds trust.

It reminds the lonely that they are not forgotten.

It turns strangers into family and wounds into windows for grace.

In a Church tempted by abstraction, proximity is incarnational.

It is not theology alone—it is theology embodied.

It is not doctrine alone—it is doctrine demonstrated.

It is not just preaching about love—it is practicing it in proximity.

Jesus did not love from afar.

He did not send sympathy from heaven—He stepped into suffering.

He did not remain distant—He drew near.

He moved toward the hurting—not away.

He touched the untouchable—lepers, the bleeding, the broken.

He sat with the outcast—tax collectors, sinners, the rejected.

He walked with the weary disciples, crowds, and the poor in spirit.

He wept with the grieving—at Lazarus's tomb, in Gethsemane, on the cross.

This is the power of proximity.

It is the ministry of presence over performance.

Of closeness over control.

Of relationship over reputation.

It is the ministry that says:

"I will not love you from a distance."

"I will not serve you from a stage."

"I will not comfort you from a script."

Let us be that Church.

Let us move toward the margins.

Let us dwell in the mess.

Let us sit with the grieving.

Let us walk with the weary.

Let us touch the untouchable.

Because when the Church chooses proximity—Jesus is revealed.

And when Jesus is revealed—***Hope is Reborn***.

Proximity Is the Posture of Christ

The incarnation is the ultimate act of proximity.

It is not just a theological truth—it is a divine descent.

It is not just a doctrine—it is a demonstration.

God did not remain abstract—He became accessible.

He did not send a messenger—He became the message.

He did not offer distant sympathy—He entered human suffering.

God did not send a message—He sent Himself.

He did not write His love in the sky—He wrote it in skin.

He did not stay in the heavens—He stepped into history.

He did not remain distant—He became flesh and dwelt among us (John 1:14).

He moved into the neighborhood.

He walked our roads.

He breathed our air.

He bore our burdens.

Jesus did not wait for people to come to Him—He went to them.

He crossed boundaries.

He broke barriers.

He defied expectations.

He went to the woman at the well—a Samaritan, a scandal, a seeker (John 4:4–26).

He met her in her shame and offered her living water.

He went to the man born blind—not just to heal his eyes, but to restore his dignity (John 9:1–7).

He saw him before anyone else did.

He went to the leper who cried out—touching what others avoided, restoring what others rejected (Mark 1:40–42).

He did not recoil—He reached.

He went to the disciples on the stormy sea—walking on water, calming chaos, speaking peace (Mark 6:47–51).

He did not wait for the storm to pass—He entered it.

This is the proximity of Christ.

It is not passive—it is pursuing.

It does not wait—it moves.

It does not observe—it intervenes.

Proximity is not convenient—it is costly.

It interrupts schedules.

It dismantles comfort.

It demands presence when presence is painful.

Proximity is not safe—it is sacrificial.

It risks rejection.

It embraces vulnerability.

It chooses incarnation over insulation.

This is the proximity we are called to embody.

Not just to preach about Jesus, but to move like Him.

To go to the wells, the streets, the prisons, the shelters.

To touch the untouchable.

To walk into storms.

To dwell among those the world avoids.

Let us be that Church.

Let us carry the incarnation into every corner of culture.

Let us move toward the margins, the mess, the mourning.

Because when the Church chooses proximity—Jesus is revealed.

And when Jesus is revealed—***Hope is Reborn***.

Proximity Is the Practice of the Church

The early Church understood proximity.

They did not build walls—they built tables.

They did not isolate—they integrated.

They did not gather for spectacle—they gathered for substance.

Their ministry was not distant—it was daily.

Not abstract—it was embodied.

They broke bread in homes—not just to eat, but to commune.

Every meal was a moment of ministry.

Every table was an altar.

Every home became a sanctuary of grace.

They shared possessions—not out of obligation, but out of overflow.

They did not measure generosity by percentages, but by proximity.

They saw needs and responded—not with pity, but with partnership.

They met daily—not because they had to, but because they wanted to.

Because proximity was their posture.

Because presence was their power.

Because the Spirit moved not just in sermons, but in shared life.

They rejoiced and mourned together (Acts 2:42–47).

They did not celebrate in isolation.

They did not grieve alone.

They entered each other's stories.

They carried each other's seasons.

They became a body—not just in belief, but in behavior.

They did not outsource compassion to programs.

They did not delegate mercy to ministries.

They lived it.

They embodied it.

They understood that proximity is not a strategy—it is a sacrifice.

Paul writes,

"Carry each other's burdens, and in this way you will fulfill the law of Christ" (Galatians 6:2, NIV).

To carry a burden, you must be close enough to feel its weight.

To share a sorrow, you must be near enough to hear the cry.

To offer hope, you must be present enough to see the need.

This is the power of proximity.

It is not efficient—but it is eternal.

It is not glamorous—but it is glorious.

It is not scalable—but it is sacred.

Let us be that Church.

Let us break bread in homes.

Let us share what we have.

Let us meet often and love deeply.

Let us rejoice and mourn together.

Let us carry burdens—not from a distance, but from within.

Because when the Church draws near—Jesus is revealed.

And when Jesus is revealed—***Hope is Reborn***.

Proximity Is the Power of the Gospel

The Gospel is not just a message—it is a movement of proximity.

It moves toward the sinner.

Toward the suffering.

Toward the forgotten.

It does not wait for perfection—it meets people in their pain.

It does not demand credentials—it offers compassion.

It does not require distance—it invites **dwelling**.

When the Church chooses proximity:

- Walls fall.
- Wounds heal.
- Hope rises.

This is the power of proximity.

It is not flashy, but it is faithful.

It is not loud, but it is lasting.

It is not distant, but it is divine.

Let us be that Church.

Let us move toward the margins.

Let us dwell in the mess.

Let us carry the name of Jesus—not as a concept, but as a **companion**.

Because when the Church draws near—**Jesus is revealed**.

And when Jesus is revealed—***Hope is Reborn***.

Bibliography

1. Holy Bible, New International Version. Scriptures cited: John 1:14; John 4:4–26; John 9:1–7; Mark 1:40–42; Mark 6:47–51; Acts 2:42–47; Galatians 6:2.

2. Bonhoeffer, Dietrich. *Life Together*. Harper & Row, 1954.

3. Nouwen, Henri J.M. *The Wounded Healer: Ministry in Contemporary Society*. Image Books, 1979.

4. Keller, Timothy. *Ministries of Mercy: The Call of the Jericho Road*. P&R Publishing, 1997.

5. Claiborne, Shane. *The Irresistible Revolution: Living as an Ordinary Radical*. Zondervan, 2006.

6. Tisby, Jemar. *How to Fight Racism: Courageous Christianity and the Journey Toward Racial Justice*. Zondervan, 2021.

7. Barna Group. "Faith in Action: How Churches Can Be a Catalyst for Community Renewal." Barna Research, 2023.

Epilogue: A Letter to the Church

A Prophetic Charge for a People of Presence

Dear Church,

We write to you not as critics, but as kin.

Not to condemn, but to **call forth**.

Not to shame, but to **summon**.

Because the world is still asking,

"Where's the Church?"

And too often, the answer is silence.

We've heard the ache in Lisa's voice.

We've read her letter—the one written in grief, in anger, in longing.

She wrote from the waiting room.

From the shelter.

From the pew she left behind.

She wrote with tears in her eyes and hope slipping through her fingers.

But today, we write a new letter.

A **response**.

A **reversal**.

A **resurrection**.

To the Leaders:

This is your moment.

Not to build bigger stages, but to build deeper wells.

Not to manage crowds, but to shepherd souls.

Not to protect platforms, but to pursue the poor, the grieving, the forgotten.

Preach the Gospel—but **live it louder**.

Lead with courage—but **kneel with compassion**.

Organize the Church—but **mobilize the Body**.

You are not the CEOs of spiritual corporations.

You are stewards of sacred presence.

You are called to proximity, not prestige.

To incarnation, not insulation.

To the Members:

You are not spectators.

You are not consumers.

You are **ministers of mercy**, every one of you.

You carry the Spirit.

You carry the name.

You carry the light.

You do not need a microphone to preach.

You do not need a title to serve.

You do not need a degree to disciple.

You just need to **show up**.

In the mess.

In the margins.

In the mundane.

Because the Church is not a building you attend.

It is a **body you become**.

To the Seekers:

We see you.

We hear you.

We believe you.

You've been hurt.

You've been overlooked.

You've been told to clean up before you come in.

But here is the truth:

Jesus meets you **in the mess**.

He walks with you **in the questions**.

He welcomes you **as you are**.

And if the Church has failed to reflect that—

we repent.

We lament.

And we recommit to being the kind of Church that looks like **Him**.

A Rewritten Letter from Lisa

Dear Church,

I almost gave up on you.

I almost walked away for good.

I was tired of the silence.

Tired of the distance.

Tired of the performance.

But then… you showed up.

You did not fix everything.

You did not have all the answers.

But you were there.

In the waiting room.

In the shelter.

In the silence.

You listened.

You wept.

You stayed.

And in your presence, I saw **His**.

In your tears, I felt **His**.

In your embrace, I heard **His voice** say,

"I am still here." I never left."

Thank you for becoming the Church I had almost stopped believing in.

Thank you for answering the question before I had to ask it.

With hope,

Lisa

Final Call

Let us be that Church.

The Church that does not wait for the cry—

but listens for the silence.

The Church that does not wait for the question—

but lives the answer.

Let us be the Church that **answers the question before it is asked**.

Let us be the Church that shows up.

That stays.

That heals.

That hopes.

Because when the Church shows up—**Jesus is revealed**.

And when Jesus is revealed—***Hope is Reborn***.

Amen.

Closing Statement

Let Us Be the Answer

The question has been asked.

In shelters and sanctuaries.

In protests and prayer circles.

In silence and in sorrow.

"Where's the Church?"

And now, the response must rise.

Not as a slogan, but as a **sacrifice**.

Not as a performance, but as **presence**.

Not as a theory, but as **testimony**.

Let us be the Church that does not wait for the cry.

Let us be the Church that listens for the silence.

Let us be the Church that moves toward the margins,

dwells in the mess,

and stays in the storm.

Let us be the Church that answers the question before it is asked.

With proximity.

With compassion.

With incarnational love.

Because when the Church shows up—**Jesus is revealed**.

And when Jesus is revealed—***Hope is Reborn***.

So, rise, Church.

Not to dominate, but to **dwell**.

Not to impress, but to **intercede**.

Not to retreat, but to **remain**.

Here we are.

And here we stay.

Until every cry is met with comfort.

Until every wound is met with witness.

Until every question is met with the presence of Christ.

Amen.

www.ingramcontent.com/pod-product-compliance
Lightning Source LLC
Chambersburg PA
CBHW040758120726
48005CB00012B/1227